THE WORLD ALMANAC
ODDBALL ANIMALS

World Almanac books may be purchased in bulk at special discounts for sales promotion, corporate gifts, fundraising, or educational purposes. Special editions can also be created to specifications. For details, contact the Special Sales Department, 307 West 36th Street, 11th Floor, New York, NY 10018 or info@skyhorsepublishing.com.

Published by World Almanac for Kids™ and World Almanac Books, an imprint of Skyhorse Publishing, Inc., 307 West 36th Street, 11th Floor, New York, NY 10018. The World Almanac® is a registered trademark of Skyhorse Publishing, Inc.® All rights reserved.

www.skyhorsepublishing.com

Please follow our publisher Tony Lyons on Instagram @tonylyonsisuncertain.

10 9 8 7 6 5 4 3 2 1

Library of Congress Cataloging-in-Publication Data is available on file.

Text by Joanne Mattern
Cover design by Kai Texel
Interior layout by Chris Schultz
Cover and interior images by Shutterstock and Getty Images unless noted.

Images under a Creative Commons license: page 13, committee: James Hassell, Smithsonian's National Zoo; page 180, blobfish: Alaska Fisheries Science Center, NOAA; page 183, black dragonfish: Naturalis Biodiversity Center, Netherlands, via Global Biodiversity Information Facility.

Print ISBN: 978-1-5107-8075-0
Ebook ISBN: 978-1-5107-8076-7

Printed in China

THE WORLD ALMANAC

ODDBALL ANIMALS

2,501

FANTASTIC FACTS

ABOUT THE WEIRDEST, WACKIEST, AND WILDEST CREATURES ON EARTH

JOANNE MATTERN

WORLD ALMANAC BOOKS

contents

THE WORLD ALMANAC

ODDBALL ANIMALS

INTRODUCTION

You've probably seen lots of animals in your life, and many may seem pretty ordinary. All animals are special in their own way, but some are much more special than others. And by "special," we mean that they have traits and behaviors that are downright weird!

Animals eat, drink, sleep, poop, walk, swim, fly, defend themselves, have babies … all the usual stuff. However, some animals take these behaviors to the extreme! And while most animals have the same basic body parts, there are some wild creatures that are born with body parts that are truly, fascinatingly outrageous.

Outrageous, oddball, weird, unusual … that's what this book is all about! We've chosen more than 150 of the wackiest animals on the planet, so turn the pages and jump in for a wild ride. You'll discover animals that shoot nasty poison from their butts, creatures that eat bones (or worse), males raising babies in their mouths, monkeys with big noses that make a big noise, and much, much more. You name it, it's all here, from Z to A.

Z to A? Don't most lists go from A to Z?

Yes, of course, but there's nothing oddball about that! We wanted to do things a little differently, so we've organized this book backward. Of course, you can jump in and read the entries in any order you like. Nothing is too off-the-wall here!

ZOMBIE WORM

1. Zombies in legends and other made-up stories eat brains. This zombie eats bones!

2. The zombie worm lives on the ocean floor, about 10,000 feet (3,048 meters) below the surface.

3. There are about 30 different species of zombie worms, found all over the world.

4. These tiny worms cover the skeletons of dead whales that fall to the bottom of the sea.

5. They produce an acid that dissolves bone.

6. Scientists first discovered zombie worms in 2002.

7. Their scientific name is Osedax.

8. *Osedax* means "bone devourer" in Latin.

9. Zombie worms look more like plants than animals.

10. They are shaped like a tube with roots at one end and a red "feather" at the other.

11. Females are about as long as your middle finger.

12. Males are smaller than an eyelash.

13. Male zombie worms don't eat bones.

14. Instead, they live inside the female and are only there to fertilize her eggs.

15. Zombie worms have been around since the days of the dinosaurs.

1. Wood frogs are the only frogs that live north of the Arctic Circle.

2. To get through the bitter-cold winters, wood frogs actually freeze solid.

3. Even though the frog's organs are encased in ice, the frog doesn't die.

4. That's because its liver produces a lot of glucose, which keeps ice from damaging the cells in the frog's body.

5. Wood frogs hold in their pee for the eight months they are frozen.

6. A chemical called urea in the pee helps the frog's body stay frozen without damage.

7. Wood frogs spend the winter under leaves on the forest floor.

8. They are the first frogs to wake up in the spring.

9. The first part of the frog's body to thaw is its heart.

10. Females lay up to 3,000 eggs at one time.

WOOD FROG

WOMBAT

1. Wombats live in Australia.

2. They are marsupials.

3. Marsupials are mammals that develop differently than other mammals.

4. When a wombat baby is born, it is tiny and helpless.

5. The baby crawls into a pouch on its mom's belly.

6. The baby stays in the pouch for seven to ten months.

7. Wombats are about 3 feet (1 meter) long.

8. That's about the same as a medium-sized dog.

9. They weigh up to 88 pounds (40 kg).

10. Wombats are nocturnal.

11. They sleep in burrows during the day and come out at night to find food.

12. Wombats are great at digging.

13. They have big paws with flat, sharp claws.

14. A wombat's burrow can have many entrances and rooms.

15. Wombats sometimes come out during the day to sunbathe.

16. A wombat's poop is shaped like a cube.

17. They use their poop to mark their territories.

18. The square shape keeps the poop from rolling away.

19. They poop up to 100 times a day.

20. Wombats are herbivores. They only eat grass.

21. Wombats are fast runners! They can zoom along at up to 25 miles per hour (40 km per hour).

22. But they can only run that fast for about 90 seconds.

23. Watch out! A charging wombat can even knock over a person!

24. Wombats can jump over 3-foot-high (1-meter-high) fences.

25. Herds of giant wombats roamed Australia in prehistoric times.

26. These giants were about the size of a rhinoceros.

27. Unlike other marsupials, a wombat's pouch faces backward.

28. That protects the babies from getting dirt thrown all over them when Mom digs.

29. There are three species of wombats.

30. October 22 is World Wombat Day.

1. There are several different species of wolf fish.

2. Some are small, measuring only about 10 inches (25 cm) long.

3. The giant wolf fish can grow up to several feet (1 meter) long.

4. Giant wolf fish live in South America's Amazon River.

5. The giant wolf fish is a vicious predator.

6. It feeds on smaller fish.

7. The giant wolf fish even eats piranhas!

8. This fish has a row of long, sharp teeth that stick out of its mouth.

9. It also has a second set of teeth in its throat.

10. There isn't a lot of oxygen in the Amazon River. So wolf fish can rise to the surface and gulp air.

11. They can also move short distances over land.

12. Some people keep wolf fish as pets. But this is not a great idea.

WOLF FISH

WOBBEGONG

1. This shark with a funny name lives in the waters off Australia.

2. They are also called carpet sharks because they lie on the bottom of the sea and look like a carpet.

3. The wobbegong's scientific name roughly translates to "well-fringed nose with shaggy beard."

4. This shark's odd appearance provides excellent camouflage.

5. Its prey can't see the shark as it lies on the sea bottom.

6. Wobbegongs eat small octopuses, crabs, and lobsters.

7. This shark senses prey is near using sensory organs called barbels.

8. A wobbegong has a big mouth.

9. It can swallow prey almost as big as the shark itself.

10. If the prey is too big to swallow, the wobbegong holds it in its mouth until it dies. Then it eats the animal in big chunks.

11. Wobbegongs have terrible eyesight.

12. They sleep during the day and hunt at night.

13. Wobbegongs have up to 20 babies, or pups, in a litter.

14. The pups stay near their mother but can take care of themselves.

WHALE-HEADED STORK

1. This bird is also called the shoebill stork.

2. It stands about 4.5 feet (1.4 meters) tall.

3. Its big bill is about 7.5 inches (19 cm) long.

4. The stork can fill its bill with tasty fish to eat.

5. It also eats snakes and even baby crocodiles.

6. The stork stands in shallow water, looking for its prey.

7. When it spots something to eat, it spears the animal with a sharp point on the end of its beak.

8. Whale-headed storks really don't like each other. They stand about 65 feet (20 meters) apart when they are feeding.

9. Even stork chicks hate each other. The largest chick sometimes kills its brothers and sisters.

10. As soon as the young chick can take care of itself, its mother kicks it out of the nest.

11. Whale-headed storks live in Africa.

12. They barely fly, and only over short distances.

WHALE SHARK

1. Is it a whale or is it a shark? The correct answer is shark.

2. This fish got its name because it is as big as some whales.

3. It is the largest shark and the largest fish.

4. A whale shark can be up to 65 feet (20 meters) long.

5. It is also a filter feeder, just like whales.

6. Whale sharks eat tiny food called krill, as well as baby shrimp and fish larvae.

7. They swallow lots of water as they swim, then filter out the food.

8. Whale sharks have about 3,000 teeth.

9. But their teeth are small, and they do not chew their food.

10. A whale shark's skeleton is made of cartilage, not bone.

11. These sharks live in warm ocean waters.

12. Whale sharks don't mind people. Scuba divers can swim right next to them without any problems.

WATER STRIDER

1. Can an insect really walk on water? The water strider can!

2. These insects live in ponds and marshes in North America.

3. They are part of a group called true bugs.

4. A true bug's mouth is shaped like a straw.

5. But back to walking on water. The water strider can do this because it has thousands of tiny hairs on its long, thin legs.

6. These hairs repel water and hold on to air.

7. The captured air helps the bug walk on the surface of the water.

8. They use their front legs to grab food, such as insects, that have fallen into the water.

9. These bugs usually live and hunt in large groups.

10. Water striders are less than an inch (2.5 cm) long.

11. Scientists are studying water striders' legs to learn how to make materials that repel water.

5

1. Vultures make the world cleaner. They are scavengers who eat carrion.

2. Carrion is the remains of dead animals, and it is a vulture's favorite food.

3. Sometimes vultures will kill sick or dying animals.

4. Vultures feed in big groups.

5. A group of vultures is sometimes called a committee.

6. A vulture's bald head helps it keep cool.

7. It also helps the bird keep its head clean when feeding on rotting animals.

8. Strong acid in a vulture's stomach helps it avoid getting food poisoning.

9. That acid can also be a weapon. A vulture will vomit its stomach acid onto a predator.

10. Vultures have a gross way of keeping cool. They pee on their legs!

11. Vultures soar instead of flapping their wings as they fly to conserve energy.

12. Vultures are divided into two groups.

13. Old World vultures live in Africa, Asia, and Europe.

14. They find their food by sight.

15. New World vultures live in North and South America.

16. They use their sense of smell to find food.

VULTURE

VAMPIRE BAT

1. Did vampire bats get their name because they suck blood? You bet they did!

2. Vampire bats live in Central and South America.

3. They live in both rainforests and deserts.

4. Vampire bats roost in caves, old mines, abandoned buildings, and rotted trees during the day.

5. At night, they come out to feed on blood.

6. These bats locate their prey by hearing them breathe.

7. Vampire bats have sharp fangs.

8. They use them to bite their prey.

9. A special chemical in the bat's blood stops the blood from clotting.

10. Then the bat laps up the blood until it has its fill.

11. Vampire bats used to prey on wild animals while they slept.

12. However, today they prey on domestic cattle, pigs, and sheep.

13. Since their prey is sleeping, the animals don't usually feel the vampire bat's bite.

14. But vampire bats can spread disease.

15. However, these bats aren't all bad.

16. Scientists are studying their blood to develop a new medicine.

17. The medicine is called Draculin after Count Dracula, the most famous vampire.

18. It could be used to stop blood clots and strokes.

19. Vampire bats are very small. They only measure about 2 inches (5 cm) long and weigh about 1 ounce (28 grams).

20. There are three different species of vampire bat.

21. Vampire bats can walk and run, and even jump!

22. Vampire bats roost in big groups called colonies.

23. A bat will die if it goes more than two days without blood.

24. Sometimes a bat will throw up blood and share it with another bat.

25. Vampire bats also groom each other with their claws.

ODDBALL

FAST FACTS!

DANGER!
10 DEADLY ANIMALS

1. **Great White Shark:** Giant mouth, check. More than 300 teeth, check. A reputation for attacking and killing people, check! Although shark attacks are rare, there's no denying these carnivores are scary—and deadly.

2. **Cape Buffalo:** When your nickname is "the Black Death," you know you're dangerous. These animals weigh up to 1,700 pounds (770 kg), stand 6 feet (1.8 meters) tall, and have horns that are 5 feet (1.5 meters) long. And they will not hesitate to charge. These bad boys kill about 200 people every year in Africa.

3. **Brazilian Wandering Spider:** You'd better hope this spider doesn't wander too close to you. Here's a clue to how dangerous they are: The spider's Latin name means "murderess." One bite filled with this spider's powerful venom can easily kill a person.

4. **Hippopotamus:** Sure, these animals are big and heavy. But dangerous? You'd better believe it! They will do just about anything to protect their territory, and that includes charging at people and baring their long, sharp tusks. Reports blame hippos for several thousand deaths each year.

5. **Rhinoceros:** What happens when you combine sharp horns, bad eyesight, and a short temper? You can end up with this deadly animal charging toward you. The best way to stay safe around rhinos is to stay away.

6. **Saltwater Crocodile:** All crocs are dangerous, but the saltwater crocodile is the scariest. They are the largest members of the crocodile family, but that's not the scariest part. The most dangerous part of this animal is its jaws. It's almost impossible to open a saltwater crocodile's mouth once it has closed its jaws. And this animal has so many sharp teeth, it literally tears its prey—which can include people—apart.

7. **Box Jellyfish:** Each tentacle on the box jellyfish is filled with thousands of tiny, poison-filled darts. That poison is strong enough to stop a person's heart. About 20 to 40 people die from box jellyfish stings every year.

8. **Tsetse Fly:** Even a little fly can spell big danger. The tsetse fly spreads nasty diseases like sleeping sickness. Despite pesticides and medicine, thousands of people in Africa still die from sleeping sickness each year.

9. **Black Mamba:** This most dangerous of snakes has very powerful venom that is almost 100 percent deadly. If a person sees this snake open its mouth to strike, he or she could be dead in about 20 minutes.

10. **Mosquito:** Believe it or not, this annoying insect has killed more people throughout history than all wars combined. That's because a bite from a mosquito can spread many different diseases, including malaria and yellow fever. These diseases still kill more than a million people a year, mostly in Africa and Asia.

TUBE WORM

1. Tube worms live deep in the ocean.

2. They live near hydrothermal vents.

3. These vents are like hot springs on the ocean floor.

4. They form where seawater meets hot magma under the surface.

5. Tube worms feed on the minerals coming out of the vents.

6. Bacteria in their bodies convert the minerals into food.

7. Tube worms have no mouths.

8. Tube worms are the largest worms in the world.

9. They can measure more than 9 feet (3 meters) long.

10. A tube worm's gills look like giant feathers.

11. Sometimes these gills attract predators, such as vent crabs.

12. If a vent crab comes too close, the worm will pull its gills into its tubelike body to hide them.

13. Scientists didn't discover these worms until 1977.

14. They think tube worms can live between 100 and 300 years.

1. These spiders get their name from the way they trap their prey.

2. They build burrows under the ground.

3. At the top of the burrow is a tiny trapdoor made of dirt and plant material.

4. The trapdoor is attached to the burrow by a thread of the spider's sticky silk.

5. When an insect walks over the hidden door, the spider senses the vibrations.

6. It quickly pulls the door open and drags its victim inside.

7. These spiders sometimes eat snakes, baby birds, and even small lizards and mice.

8. A trapdoor spider is about 1.5 inches (4 cm) long.

9. Like most spiders, they have 8 eyes.

10. Most spiders do not care for their young, but the trapdoor spider keeps her eggs safe in a special room inside her burrow.

11. When the eggs hatch, Mama Spider brings them food until the spiderlings are big enough to go out on their own.

12. Trapdoor spiders live in warm places all over the world.

TRAPDOOR SPIDER

THORNY DEVIL

1. This spiky lizard gets its name from the horns on top of its head. They look like the horns of a devil or a dragon.

2. The thorny devil is also called the mountain devil, thorny lizard, and thorny dragon.

3. All those spikes protect the lizard from predators.

4. The thorny lizard has a "false head." Markings on the back of its neck look like another head.

5. The lizard will display its false head to predators to confuse them.

6. Thorny devils can also roll themselves into a spiky ball to discourage anything from eating them.

7. These lizards live in hot deserts and scrublands in Australia.

8. They are active during the day.

9. Thorny lizards eat insects. They can eat thousands of ants in a day.

10. Males bob their heads and wave their legs around to attract females.

11. Females lay 3 to 10 eggs in an underground burrow.

12. The baby lizards can take care of themselves right after they hatch.

TERMITE

1. There are more than 2,000 species of termites.
2. These insects live all over the world.
3. Some species build huge mounds for their homes.
4. A mound can be up to 17 feet (5 meters) tall.
5. These mounds can contain hundreds of rooms.
6. A group of termites is called a colony.
7. Thousands of termites can live in one colony.
8. Each colony has one queen.
9. The queen's only job is to lay eggs.
10. A queen can lay 30,000 eggs a day.
11. As the queen produces eggs, she gets so big she can't move.
12. The other termites take care of their huge queen.
13. Termites are bad news to homeowners.
14. They like to chew on wood.
15. Termites cause more than $5 billion worth of damage each year.

TEAR-DRINKING MOTH

1. This insect's name says it all. Yes, it really does drink tears.

2. These moths land on birds while they are sleeping.

3. Then they stick their long tongue into the bird's eyeball to lap up its tears.

4. Surprisingly, the birds don't seem to mind!

5. They actually sleep through the whole experience.

6. These moths drink tears to get salt into their diet.

7. They may also get protein from the animal tears.

8. Tear-drinking moths are part of the tiger moth family.

9. These insects can be as long as a person's fist.

10. They live in warm climates in South America, Africa, and Asia.

TAWNY FROGMOUTH

1. This bird has a really big mouth!

2. It got its name because its mouth looks like a frog's mouth.

3. They use their big mouths to catch prey.

4. A sharp hook at the end of its beak helps the bird snag its food.

5. They eat insects, fish, amphibians, and crustaceans.

6. Tawny frogmouths live in Australia and Tasmania.

7. They have short, weak legs.

8. They usually hunt by sitting still, then ambushing prey when it comes too close.

9. Although they look a bit like owls, these birds are actually part of a bird family called nightjars.

10. Tawny frogmouths hiss or buzz when they are startled.

TASMANIAN DEVIL

1. That wild, snarling, crazy critter in the old cartoons is actually real!

2. The Tasmanian devil lives on the Australian island of Tasmania.

3. It is the largest carnivorous marsupial.

4. These animals eat meat and only meat.

5. Rabbits, wombats, and wallabies are their favorite food.

6. Tasmanian devils also eat carrion (dead animals).

7. They will even eat the bones and fur of a dead animal.

8. Sometimes they will take a nap inside the dead animal they are eating.

9. When they wake up, they can get right back to eating!

10. This animal can eat up to 40 percent of its body weight in one day.

11. Tasmanian devils have an excellent sense of smell.

12. They have great eyesight too.

13. These senses help them find their prey.

14. This creature is the size of a small dog.

15. It is actually kind of cute—until it opens its mouth.

16. Tasmanian devils have a strong jaw and a mouthful of very sharp teeth.

17. Their bite is one of the most powerful on Earth.

18. Their bite is strong enough to crush bone and bite through metal.

19. When it is threatened, the Tasmanian devil will lunge at its attacker with its teeth bared.

20. It will also howl, shriek, and spin around, just like its cartoon character.

21. They do the same things when they want to impress a mate.

22. Tasmanian devils are active at night.

23. During the day they sleep in hollow logs, burrows, or caves.

24. Mama devils give birth to 20 to 40 babies at a time.

25. The babies are called joeys.

26. A baby Tasmanian devil is only the size of a raisin.

27. The babies crawl up their mother's fur and into her pouch. That's when things get rough.

28. A female Tasmanian devil only has four teats in her pouch. That means only four of the babies can nurse—and survive.

29. Tasmanian devils store fat in their tails.

30. These animals are fast runners and good swimmers.

TARSIER

1. These little critters are part of a group called primates.

2. Unlike other primates, tarsiers eat meat, not plants.

3. Insects, lizards, and snakes are their favorite food.

4. Tarsiers wait in trees to ambush their prey.

5. They can snatch a bird or bat right out of the air.

6. Tarsiers live in the Philippines and other islands in Southeast Asia.

7. They are only 3.5 to 6 inches (9 to 16 cm) long.

8. Their tails are twice as long as their bodies.

9. Their back legs are much longer than their front ones.

10. Tarsiers weigh between 3 and 5 ounces (85 to 170 grams).

11. These animals live in trees.

12. They use their long fingers to cling to the tree.

13. They also press their tail against the tree for balance.

14. They are great at leaping from branch to branch.

15. Tarsiers are active at night.

16. A big part of their brain processes visual stimuli.

17. These animals have big eyes too.

18. Their eyes are the largest relative to body size of any mammal.

19. Those big eyes and the big part of its brain help the tarsier see its prey in the dark.

20. A tarsier's eyes are so large, they can't rotate them.

21. Instead, this animal rotates its head 180 degrees.

22. Tarsiers talk to each other by making high-pitched sounds.

23. These sounds help males and females find each other.

24. They also help the animals defend their territory against other tarsiers.

25. Baby tarsiers are born with their eyes open.

26. They can climb trees just an hour after birth.

TARDIGRADE

1. These creatures are often called water bears because of the way they look.

2. Tardigrades are super-tiny. They are smaller than a poppy seed, so you need a microscope to get a good look at them.

3. These creatures may be tiny, but they are extremely tough.

4. You can boil, freeze, crush, or dehydrate tardigrades, but they will still survive.

5. They have even survived being blasted into space!

6. A Russian space mission sent tardigrades into space in 2007.

7. Tardigrades need just a drop of water to survive.

8. If there is no water, these creatures crawl into a ball and go into a deep hibernation—sometimes for years.

9. Tardigrades have sharp claws and teeth.

10. They use their teeth to suck juice out of moss and algae.

11. These creatures live almost everywhere on Earth, from high mountain peaks to tropical oceans.

12. They have been around for 600 million years.

TARANTULA HAWK

1. This creature is not a tarantula or a hawk.

2. It is actually a wasp.

3. They live in every continent except Europe and Antarctica.

4. In the United States, they live in the southwestern deserts.

5. These wasps can be up to 2 inches (5 cm) long.

6. Tarantula hawks have bright blue bodies and bright orange wings.

7. Usually, these wasps feed on flower nectar.

8. However, adult females hunt tarantulas—the spiders, that is.

9. A female will sting a tarantula to paralyze it. Then they bring the tarantula back to the nest.

10. In the nest, the wasp lays an egg in the tarantula's abdomen.

11. They she covers the entrance to the burrow, trapping the tarantula inside.

12. When the egg hatches, the larvae will feed on the still-living tarantula for several weeks.

13. Only female tarantula hawks have stingers.

14. A sting from a tarantula hawk is very painful.

15. One scientist described what to do if you are stung: "Lie down and scream."

TARANTULA

1. This big spider gets its name from Taranto, Italy.

2. About 500 years ago, some people in Taranto came down with a strange "dancing sickness."

3. Many people believed the illness was caused by a bite from the large spiders that lived in the area.

4. Tarantulas live on every continent except Antarctica, but most live in South America.

5. Tarantulas look like they are covered with hair. But the covering is actually more like bristles, and it is made of a fiber called chitin.

6. Some tarantulas can fling their bristles at enemies to scare them away.

7. Each bristle has a sharp barb on the end that can stick in the predator's eyes or snout. Ouch!

8. Tarantulas don't spin webs to catch their prey.

9. Instead, they jump out and grab it.

10. Most tarantulas eat insects and small invertebrates (animals without backbones).

11. Larger tarantulas eat frogs, lizards, and mice.

12. The largest tarantula is South America's Goliath birdeater.

13. This spider measures 11 inches (28 cm) across and is the largest spider in the world.

14. Despite its name and size, the Goliath birdeater doesn't eat birds.

15. Tarantulas shed their outer skin as they grow.

16. They can also grow new internal organs and new legs.

TAPIR

1. Tapirs have a funny face. You notice their big nose right away.

2. A tapir's long nose is *prehensile*. That means it can be used to grab things.

3. A tapir uses its nose to grab fruit and leaves to eat.

4. Tapirs are great swimmers.

5. They hold their nose above the water like a snorkel to breathe.

6. Tapirs are the largest native land mammals in South America.

7. They weigh between 300 and 700 pounds (136 to 318 kg).

8. Tapirs are living fossils.

9. They have been around since the Eocene era, 56 million years ago.

10. Tapirs have four toes on their front feet and three toes on their back feet.

11. They can run fast over short distances.

12. A tapir's skin, or hide, is quite tough.

13. Baby tapirs are spotted and striped to camouflage them from predators.

ODDBALL

FAST FACTS!

20 WEIRD WAYS ANIMALS SLEEP

1. Only half of a dolphin's brain is asleep at a time. The other half stays awake to watch for danger.

2. Dolphins float on the surface so they can breathe while they are sleeping.

3. Sharks also need to keep moving as they sleep, so their gills can remove oxygen from water.

4. Scientists observed a great white shark facing into the current while it slept, so the water would flow over its gills.

5. Sperm whales float vertically while they sleep.

6. Sea otters often hold paws while they sleep.

7. They also wrap themselves in seaweed to stay together during naptime.

8. Elephants nap for a few minutes at a time, and they usually sleep standing up.

9. Horses also usually sleep standing up, thanks to an ability to lock their legs into place so they don't fall over.

10. Sometimes a walrus will anchor itself while it sleeps by sticking a tusk into an ice floe.

5

11. Walruses can also go for up to 3½ days without sleeping.

12. Large groups of bats hang upside-down while they sleep.

13. It's hard not to be seen while you're sleeping when you're a giraffe. These tall mammals only doze off for a few minutes at a time.

14. Sometimes a giraffe will lie down and rest its head on its back, but usually these animals sleep standing up.

15. Great frigatebirds only sleep in 7- to 12-second bursts while they fly.

16. Ducks sleep in rows. The ducks on the outside edge keep one eye open to check for danger.

17. Meerkats like to sleep in a big pile. How cozy!

18. Snails can estivate, or sleep through warm, dry months, for years.

19. Some bears give birth while they are hibernating, or sleeping through the winter.

20. Chimpanzees take a lot of time and care to build a nest high in the trees—then abandon it and build a new nest the next night!

SURINAM TOAD

1. This creature is actually a frog, not a toad.

2. It was called a toad because of its rough skin.

3. This animal is also called the star-fingered toad because each of its fingers has a star-shaped tip.

4. It lives in the Amazon rainforest.

5. The Surinam toad likes to lie still in the water.

6. Its dark color makes it look like a rock or a leaf, so predators usually swim past.

7. The Surinam toad lies still until small fish, crustaceans, or worms swim by.

8. Its fingers can sense when prey is near.

9. The toad gobbles down its prey in one bite.

10. Surinam toads do not have teeth or a tongue.

11. Females lay 60 to 100 eggs.

12. After the male fertilizes the eggs, he sticks them on the female's back.

13. Skin grows over the eggs to protect them.

14. After three or four months, tiny toadlets burst out of mom's skin and swim away.

15. But baby toadlets sometimes eat each other!

SUGAR GLIDER

1. Sugar gliders live in large colonies in Australia, Tasmania, New Guinea, and some Indonesian islands.

2. This cutie has soft, thick fur.

3. It also has stretchy skin between its legs and its body.

4. That skin stretches out to allow the sugar glider to glide from tree to tree.

5. A sugar glider can glide up to 148 feet (45 meters).

6. It can snap up a moth in mid-glide.

7. Sugar gliders also eat fruit, vegetables, nuts, and small mice.

8. An angry sugar glider makes a noise that sounds like a dog yapping.

9. A really angry sugar glider will attack!

10. These creatures have opposable thumbs and four fingers ending in a sharp claw on each hand.

11. Sugar gliders are great at hanging on branches.

12. They spend almost all of their time in the trees.

13. Male sugar gliders have a bald spot on top of their heads. That spot is actually a scent gland.

14. Like other marsupials, a female sugar glider raises its young in a pouch on its belly.

15. Some people keep sugar gliders as pets.

STONEFISH

1. These little fish pose a big threat.

2. They are the most venomous creature in the sea.

3. Stonefish measure 12 to 16 inches (30 to 40 cm) long.

4. A stonefish's venom can kill an animal—or a human!

5. It stores its venom in 13 sharp fins on its back.

6. More spines are hidden under its thick skin.

7. Stonefish are hard to see. They blend in perfectly with their surroundings.

8. Stonefish are super-fast predators.

9. They hide in the sand until shrimp or small fish swims by.

10. Then, zoom! The stonefish swallows its prey in a fraction of a second.

11. These fish live in the Pacific and Indian Oceans.

12. Stonefish can live outside of water for up to 24 hours and are sometimes found on beaches. So be careful where you step!

STINK BUG

1. Stink bugs really are stinky! They give off a powerful, skunky smell when touched.

2. The smell—and the bad taste it makes—help protect these insects from predators.

3. If smelling awful doesn't work, stink bugs also play dead to fool other animals.

4. Stink bugs originally came from Asia.

5. They came to the United States in 1996 and are now found throughout the 50 states.

6. Stinkbugs often go inside people's homes when the weather gets cold outside.

7. Although stinkbugs don't bite and aren't dangerous to people, they can do a lot of damage to farm crops.

8. Adult stink bugs can fly, but young bugs can't.

9. Young stink bugs are called nymphs.

10. Nymphs shed their outer skin four or five times as they grow bigger.

STINGRAY

1. Stingrays sure don't look like fish, but that's exactly what they are.

2. Stingrays are related to sharks.

3. Just like sharks, stingrays have cartilage instead of bones.

4. A stingray's long, wide fins give it a round shape.

5. Stingrays swim by flapping their fins or by moving their whole bodies.

6. They move at a leisurely 0.85 mile (1.35 km) per hour.

7. Some stingrays migrate distances as far as 528 miles (850 km).

8. They are carnivores and eat shrimp, oysters, crabs, and clams.

9. A stingray's eyes are on top of its head, but it doesn't really use them to find prey.

10. Instead, stingrays have special sense organs on their face called ampullae of Lorenzini.

11. These organs can sense electrical charges in the water, which helps stingrays find their prey.

12. Stingrays can also sense magnetic fields.

13. They chomp their prey with their powerful jaws.

14. A stingray's gills and mouth are on the bottom of its body.

15. A stingray defends itself with its tail.

16. Some stingrays have a sharp spiky spine in their tails.

17. Others can release venom with their tails.

18. Stingrays live in almost all the oceans in the world.

19. These creatures have been on Earth for 150 million years.

20. Female stingrays are larger and live longer than males.

21. Females can live between 15 and 22 years, while males only live five to seven years.

22. Baby stingrays can take care of themselves as soon as they are born.

23. Stingrays bury themselves in the sand when they sleep, but their dangerous tail sticks out of the sand to protect them.

24. There are more than 200 species of stingrays.

25. The largest stingray ever caught weighed 661 pounds (300 kg).

26. That bad boy was caught in the Mekong River in Cambodia.

27. In 2006, a stingray killed beloved wildlife expert Steve Irwin.

STICK INSECT

1. It's easy to see how the stick insect got its name! They look like sticks with legs.

2. They are sometimes called walking sticks.

3. Stick insects are the longest insects in the world.

4. Most measure about 12 inches (30 cm) long.

5. The longest stick insect measured 22 inches (56 cm) long with its legs extended.

6. Stick insects live in trees where there are plenty of leaves to eat.

7. Bats and birds prey on stick insects.

8. If danger approaches, a stick insect will stay very still to fool it into thinking it's a stick.

9. What if the predator grabs the stick insect's leg? No problem! The leg will break off and the insect will grow a new one.

10. There are about 3,000 species of stick insect.

11. They live in warm places all over the world.

12. Some females lay eggs that look like plant seeds to fool animals that like to eat insect eggs.

STAR-NOSED MOLE

1. This funny-looking creature has tentacles for a face!

2. Its nose is surrounded by 22 tentacles.

3. Those tentacles help the star-nosed mole find food.

4. Each tentacle is full of nerves that can sense earthworms, insects, and other prey.

5. Star-nosed moles live underground.

6. They dig through the soil looking for food.

7. Digging is easy when you have big feet and long claws like this mole does!

8. These animals are almost blind, because sight doesn't matter when you live in the dark.

9. Star-nosed moles are good swimmers.

10. They smell underwater by sucking water into their nose and blowing out bubbles.

11. They are the only species of mole that lives in swamps and marshes.

12. Star-nosed moles live in the eastern half of North America.

SQUID

1. Squids are related to octopuses.

2. You can tell the two apart by counting.

3. Octopuses and squids both have eight arms, but squids also have two long tentacles.

4. They use those tentacles to grab prey.

5. If a squid loses a tentacle, it can grow a new one.

6. A squid's mouth is in the middle of its tentacles.

7. Squids eat fish, crustaceans, and even other squids.

8. They can eat 30 percent of their body weight in a single day.

9. Squids are invertebrates, which means they have no backbone.

10. A squid's body is supported by a shell inside.

11. They are the fastest swimming invertebrates.

12. Squids swim backward.

13. They suck water in through a tube, then push it out to propel themselves through the water.

14. Squids can change color to hide from predators.

15. They also change color when looking for a mate.

16. They can also shoot out ink to scare predators away.

17. Squid have been seen fighting sharks, which are their main enemy.

18. Seals, whales, and seabirds also eat squid.

19. Squid eggs are very small.

20. Some squid attach their eggs to their bodies until the eggs hatch and others attach the eggs to rocks or corals.

21. Some squids even let the eggs float away in the water.

22. Squids are one of the largest sea creatures.

23. The colossal squid can grow up to 46 feet (14 meters) counting its body and tentacle lengths.

24. It weighs about 1,100 pounds (500 kg).

25. Colossal squid live in the waters around Antarctica.

26. Squids have the largest eye of any animal, measuring up to 106 inches (27 cm) in diameter.

27. Its pupils are 3.5 inches (9 cm) across.

28. Squids have three hearts.

29. Ancient myths about sea monsters were often based on squids.

30. Squids are very intelligent.

SPINY ORB WEB SPIDER

1. These spiders spin large, wheel-shaped webs.

2. You can spot these webs hanging between trees or from tree branches.

3. The webs catch insects for the spider to eat.

4. These spiders are only about half an inch (1 cm) long.

5. Spiny orb web spiders get their name from the sharp spines on their abdomen.

6. Only females have these spines.

7. These spiders don't hurt humans.

8. A male spider comes to the female's web to fertilize her eggs.

9. Then the female lays 100 to 200 eggs.

10. She wraps the eggs in silk to make a sac, then hangs the sac to the underside of a leaf.

11. The eggs hatch 11 to 13 days later.

SPANISH RIBBED NEWT

1. This amphibian has a WILD way to defend itself.

2. It can push its ribs out into sharp barbs along the sides of its body. Ouch!

3. At the same time, glands produce venom that coats the ribs and gets into the predator's mouth.

4. The Spanish ribbed newt is immune to its own venom.

5. A Spanish ribbed newt grows to about 12 inches (30 cm) long in the wild.

6. It is one of the largest newts.

7. They are smaller when they are raised in captivity.

8. These newts live in Spain and Morocco.

9. They live in non-moving water.

10. Females attach their eggs to the underside of underwater plants.

11. Spanish ribbed newts have been sent into space at least six times!

12. Astronauts studied how the animals reacted to microgravity.

SOFTSHELL TURTLE

1. Most turtles have a hard shell. Not these critters!

2. A softshell turtle's shell does not have the hard scutes, or scales, that other turtles have.

3. Instead, the shell, or carapace, feels more like thick leather.

4. These turtles live in fresh water around the world.

5. They like places with muddy or sandy bottoms.

6. The turtles hide in the mud.

7. Softshell turtles have webbed feet, which helps them swim.

8. A softshell has long, tube-like nostrils it can stick above the water to breathe.

9. It also has a long neck so it can stick its head far out of its shell.

10. These turtles like to hang out in the sun. They bask on logs or rocks in the water.

11. Softshell turtles eat insects, snails, and fish.

12. Sometimes they catch and eat small birds.

13. These turtles have a powerful, painful bite.

14. They can also secrete a nasty-smelling chemical if they feel scared.

SNAIL

1. Snails have more teeth than any other animal.

2. But their teeth are super-tiny.

3. Snails have up to 12,000 tiny teeth on a structure called the radula.

4. A radula looks like a tiny tongue covered with teeth.

5. They use the radula to scrape up food.

6. Snails will eat almost anything.

7. Their favorite foods are plant matter, animal poop, and even other snails.

8. Snails sleep for two to four days at a time. Then they stay awake for a whole day.

9. Snails are born with their shells.

10. As the snail grows, so does its shell.

11. Snails are super-slow. They only move about 1 foot (0.3 meters) an hour.

12. A snail has two pairs of tentacles on its head.

13. The top pair contains the snail's eyes.

14. The snail uses the bottom pair to smell and feel its way around.

15. Snails can't hear.

16. These animals leave a trail of slime behind them wherever they go.

17. During hibernation, groups of snails cover themselves in slime and glue their shells shut.

SLUG

1. Slugs and snails are members of the same family.

2. They are both gastropods, which means "stomach foot."

3. A slug's bottom side is a powerful muscle that helps the slug move.

4. Slugs do not have a shell.

5. A slug's blood is blue and most of its organs are on its right side.

6. Slugs are covered with slime and leave a trail of it behind them.

7. The slime trail helps slugs find their way back home.

8. Slugs have both male and female reproductive organs.

9. That means they can mate with themselves!

10. Slugs poop from the side of their heads.

11. Slugs lay about 100 eggs several times a year.

12. Slug eggs can stay dormant until conditions are just right for them to hatch.

13. A slug can stretch up to twenty times its length.

14. It can also squeeze its body to fit through small holes.

15. One type of slug can grow up to 1 foot (30 cm) long.

16. A slug can eat forty times its weight in one day.

SLOW LORIS

1. These primates only live in a few places in Southeast and South Asia.

2. They are nocturnal.

3. Their big eyes help them see in the dark.

4. Slow lorises often stay still for long periods of time. Their lack of movement gave them their name.

5. Slow lorises spend almost all their time in trees.

6. They only come down to the ground to poop.

7. A slow loris has a bare patch under each arm that secretes oil.

8. When it is threatened, it licks the patch to mix the oil with its saliva.

9. That mixture is venomous enough to kill small animals.

10. Their bottom front teeth are shaped like a comb.

11. They use this tooth comb to groom themselves.

12. Slow lorises are omnivores. They eat animals, plants, and nectar.

SLOTH

1. There are two kinds of sloths: two-toed sloths and three-toed sloths. You can probably guess how to tell them apart!

2. Sloths live in the rainforests of South and Central America.

3. Sloths are strong! Even a baby sloth can lift its entire body up with one arm.

4. The tendons on a sloth's arms and legs can lock into place. This lets them hang on to a branch without making any effort.

5. A sloth's grip is so strong, even a jaguar can't tear it from its tree.

6. Sloths eat tough leaves. They have a four-chambered stomach to digest the tough foliage.

7. It can take up to four weeks for food to pass through a sloth's digestive system.

8. A sloth can only eat if its stomach is empty.

9. A sloth can starve to death with a full stomach.

10. Sloths spend almost their entire lives in trees.

11. Sloths come down to the ground to poop.

12. They only poop once a week.

13. Pooping is dangerous if you're a sloth! Being on the ground makes them a good target for predators.

14. A sloth can lose one-third of its body weight in one poop.

15. A sloth cannot stand on all four feet. Its front arms are too long, and its back legs are too weak.

16. Instead, they use their strong front arms to pull themselves along in a slow crawl.

17. Sloths are excellent swimmers.

18. Sloths have been around for more than 65 million years.

19. Long ago, giant ground-dwelling sloths roamed the Earth.

20. Insects and algae live in a sloth's fur.

21. The algae on a sloth's fur gives it a green color, which helps the animal blend in with the trees.

22. Sloths fall out of trees a lot, but they rarely get hurt.

23. Sloths have terrible eyesight. They are colorblind and can't see at all in bright sunlight.

24. Three-toed sloths have two more vertebrae in their necks than any other mammal.

25. Sloths sleep up to 20 hours a day.

26. Sloths are related to armadillos and anteaters.

SKUNK

1. Skunks were once thought to be part of the same family as weasels, minks, and wolverines.

2. Then scientists studied their DNA and decided skunks were their own family.

3. That family is called Mephitidae.

4. A skunk's best defense is its stinky smell.

5. When it is threatened, it sprays a nasty-smelling liquid called musk from glands near its butt.

6. A skunk can spray a narrow stream of musk or release the liquid as a mist.

7. It can spray its musk up to 12 feet (3.6 meters).

8. Skunks often aim the spray at their predator's eyes.

9. Some skunks have cool dance moves and dance before releasing their spray.

10. Some skunks do a handstand and dance on their front legs with their back legs and tail sticking up in the air.

11. Skunks are omnivores.

12. They eat grubs, fruit, worms, mushrooms, even lizards, frogs, and small snakes.

13. A skunk's sharp claws are great at digging.

14. Skunks have been known to attack beehives and eat all the bees inside.

15. There are five different types of skunks, but all of them are black and white.

16. Some skunks are spotted, while others are striped.

17. Skunks usually nest in abandoned burrows or hollow trees or tree stumps.

18. Sometimes they nest under porches or decks, which is terrible luck for the people who live there!

19. Skunks are nocturnal, although they are sometimes seen during the day.

20. They burrow underground during the winter but do not hibernate.

21. Skunks spend almost all of their time alone.

22. A female gives birth to four to seven babies called kits every spring.

23. They stay with their mom until fall.

24. A skunk has terrible eyesight and often sprays because it is surprised.

25. Skunks can run up to 10 miles (16 km) an hour.

1. Skates are blobby-looking fish.

2. They live on the bottom of the sea in cold water.

3. They belong to the same family as stingrays.

4. A skate's skeleton is made of cartilage, not bone.

5. The largest type of skate can grow up to 8 feet (2.4 meters) long.

6. They have lots of small, pointy teeth.

7. A skate's tail is thick and has a row of spikes up the middle.

8. Skates lay their eggs in a case that is sometimes called a mermaid's purse.

9. The egg case has four sharp hooks that attach it to seaweed or other plants.

10. A skate lays between 60 and 80 eggs a year.

11. It can take up to 15 months for the eggs to hatch.

12. Some people like to cook and eat skates.

SKATE

SHRIKE

1. This cute little songbird is actually a deadly predator.

2. Shrikes sit on utility poles or fence posts where they can easily spot their prey.

3. When a shrike sees an insect, lizard, or small mammal, it attacks!

4. The shrike flies down and grabs its prey with its sharp, hooked beak.

5. The bird jabs its beak into its prey's spinal cord to paralyze it, then shakes the animal to break its neck.

6. Shrikes have an unusual way to eat poisonous animals, like some butterflies or toads.

7. To kill this prey, they impale it on a sharp thorn or piece of barbed wire.

8. After a few days, the poison is no longer dangerous, and the shrike comes back to eat.

9. Shrikes also eat the non-poisonous parts of some grasshoppers and throw the poisonous bits away.

10. A shrike will carry off prey that is bigger than itself.

11. It carries prey in its feet or on its back.

12. Their violent behavior has given shrikes the nickname "butcherbird."

SECRETARY BIRD

1. This bird looks like it could take some notes!

2. The long feathers behind its head look like the quill pens secretaries used to write with in the old days.

3. Some people think that's how this bird got its name.

4. Others think its name comes from the Arabic word "saqr et-tair," which means "hawk of the semi-desert."

5. The secretary bird is one of Africa's largest birds of prey.

6. These birds roost in trees during the night and fly down to the grass to hunt during the day.

7. Secretary birds hunt in pairs or small family groups.

8. They stalk through the grass, looking for insects and small animals to eat.

9. They strike their prey with their beaks or stomp it to death with their feet.

10. These birds are great at killing snakes! Even venomous snakes don't scare them.

11. A secretary bird's nest can be up to 8 feet (2.4 meters) wide.

12. Bird pairs usually use the same nest every year.

SEAHORSE

1. When is a horse not a horse? When it's a horse? When it's a fish! It's easy to see how this fish got its name.

2. Seahorses are covered in tiny plates.

3. They use their curved tail to hold on to sea plants.

4. A seahorse has an organ called a swim bladder that holds tiny bubbles of air.

5. It can regulate how much air is in the swim bladder, which helps the fish move up or down in the water.

6. Female seahorses lay hundreds of eggs in a pouch on the male's abdomen.

7. The males carry the eggs in this brood pouch for about 45 days.

8. After they hatch, baby seahorses are completely on their own.

9. Groups of young seahorses link their tails together and float along, looking for food.

10. Seahorses are ambush predators.

11. The seahorse stays still until a tiny crustacean swims past.

12. Then the seahorse sucks its prey into its tube-like mouth and swallows it whole.

SEA URCHIN

1. Sea urchins are part of a group called echinoderms.

2. All echinoderms have spiky skins.

3. Sea urchins live in all the world's oceans.

4. Some live between the high and low tide lines on the beach.

5. Others live deep in the ocean.

6. Sea urchins can't swim.

7. Instead, they use little tube feet to move along rocks or coral.

8. Each foot has a sucker at the tip.

9. The sea urchin pushes water in and out of its feet to move.

10. They also use their tube feet to scrape algae into their mouth.

11. That's easy to do because a sea urchin's mouth is on the bottom of its body.

12. They poop from an anus on the top of the body.

13. Most sea urchins release millions of eggs at one time.

14. The eggs float in the water or in their mother's spines until they hatch.

15. Some sea urchins have venom in their spines. Be careful not to step on one!

1. Sea stars used to be called starfish. But they aren't fish at all.

2. They are echinoderms, a group that has hard, spiny skins.

3. Starfish only live in salt water.

4. They have no blood.

5. Instead of blood, these creatures use sea water to pump nutrients through their body.

6. Sea stars use their tube feet to move and to hold on to prey.

7. Their favorite foods are clams, oysters, and snails.

8. A sea star's mouth is too small to swallow its food.

9. Instead, it pushes its stomach out through its mouth and digests its food on the spot.

10. Most sea stars have five arms, but some have up to fifty.

11. If a sea star loses an arm, it can grow a new one.

12. Sea stars don't have brains.

13. Instead, they have spots on the ends of their arms that can sense light.

SEA STAR

SEA CUCUMBER

1. The sea cucumber is an echinoderm, like the sea urchin.

2. This animal has tiny spines, called ossicles, in its skin.

3. The ossicles are so small, they can only be seen under a microscope.

4. Sea cucumbers use tube feet to move around.

5. A sea cucumber has a mouth at one end and an anus at the other.

6. A ring of tentacles surrounds the mouth and pushes food inside.

7. Sea cucumbers eat algae, plankton, and small invertebrates.

8. The sea cucumber breathes through its anus.

9. Its anus sucks water into its body, and the animal's respiratory system removes oxygen from the water.

10. Some sea cucumbers eat sediment, or the sand at the ocean bottom.

11. They digest the food inside the sediment, then excrete the sandy, nonfood parts in long strands. That's a strange way to poop!

12. If a sea cucumber feels threatened, it can push its inner organs out of its body.

13. Its organs are toxic and can poison an attacker, or at least give the sea cucumber time to get away.

14. Its inner organs will grow back.

SAILFISH

1. The sailfish is the fastest fish in the ocean.

2. This fish can zip along at 70 miles (113 km) an hour.

3. The sail on this fish's back is actually a large dorsal fin.

4. That fin helps the fish move through the water at an incredible speed.

5. They live near the surface of the ocean but will dive up to 1,150 feet (350 meters) to find food.

6. A sailfish's mouth is shaped like a long, thin bird's beak.

7. Its upper jaw is twice as long as its lower jaw.

8. Sailfish can be up to 10 feet (3 meters) long and weigh up to 220 pounds (100 kg).

9. But they are tiny when they are born, measuring $\frac{1}{8}$ inch (0.3 cm) long.

10. Adult sailfish eat large fish, crustaceans, and squid.

11. Sometimes a group of sailfish will use their dorsal fins to trap schools of fish to eat.

12. A female sailfish can release millions of eggs.

13. But most of the eggs are eaten by other animals before they can hatch.

14. A sailfish can change color. Scientists aren't sure why.

ODDBALL

1. **Dragonfly:** Average round trip: 8,700 to 11,200 miles (14,000 to 18,000 km). Some species of these super-flyers travel thousands of miles from India to southern Africa. Along the way, they stop to lay eggs in puddles.

2. **Great White Shark:** Longest migration: 12,000 miles (20,000 km). Great whites dive deep and swim slowly during migrations. Some have been recorded swimming thousands of miles between South Africa and Australia.

3. **Gray Whale:** Average round trip: 10,000 to 14,000 miles (16,000 to 22,000 km). Gray whales migrate between the chilly waters of Alaska down the warm California coast. Maybe, like people, they just want a vacation in the sun!

4. **Adélie Penguin:** Longest migration: 10,930 miles (17,600 km). These little penguins follow the sun across Antarctica. Their journey ensures that these penguins can find enough food during the long winter months.

5. **Leatherback Sea Turtle:** Average round trip: 6,200 to 9,300 miles (10,000 to 15,000 km). These huge creatures have the longest migration of any sea turtles. They start in the chilly waters around Norway and Alaska, where there is plenty of food, then travel way down south to New Zealand and southern Africa to lay their eggs on warm beaches.

6. **Bar-tailed Godwit:** Average round trip: 18,020 miles (29,000 km). This oddly named bird doesn't have time to stop for a bite. It flies more than 18,000 miles from the Arctic Sea all the way to Australia and New Zealand, without a single break for dinner. Remember that next time you're really craving a snack on a long road trip!

7. **Humpback Whale:** Average round trip: 10,000 miles (16,000 km). Like other super-migrators, humpback whales travel from cold waters with lots of food to warm waters where they give birth. They eat lots of fish as they swim from the North Pacific Ocean to build up their strength and fat reserves, then have their calves in southern waters where there are fewer predators.

8. **Wildebeest:** Average round trip: 1,000 miles (1,609 km). Anyone lucky enough to see a huge herd of wildebeest thundering across the African plains won't soon forget it. Wildebeests travel back and forth between wet and dry areas to find food, following the patterns of the rainy season.

....

9. **Monarch Butterfly:** Average round trip: 5,000 miles (8,046 km). Every year, huge swarms of these colorful butterflies journey from the northern United States and southern Canada down to Florida and Mexico. Individual butterflies don't make the whole journey. Instead, they lay eggs and die, and then their offspring continue the trip south.

....

10. **Arctic Tern:** Average round trip: 44,100 miles (70,900 km). No other animal travels as far as the Arctic tern. Each year, these birds make the long trip from northern Europe to Antarctica, experiencing two summers every year. (Seasons are reversed in the Southern Hemisphere.) These little birds weigh less than 4.5 ounces (127 grams) and use wind currents to help them along on their journey.

....

RHINOCEROS HORNBILL

1. This bird looks like it has two beaks instead of one.

2. The second beak is called a casque.

3. The casque is made of keratin—the same material as fingernails.

4. The bird's casque has one job: to make the male's mating call really loud.

5. You can tell male and female hornbills apart by their eyes.

6. A female has a white ring around her eyes, and males have red rings around theirs.

7. Hornbills mostly eat fruit, but sometimes they eat insects and small mammals too.

8. A female hornbill lays her eggs inside a hollow tree. Then she goes inside the nest, and her male partner seals up the hole with poop and mud.

9. The male passes food to the female and her chicks through a slit in the mud.

10. The female breaks out after four to five months.

11. The babies stay sealed up for a few months longer, until they can survive on their own.

12. Hornbills usually mate for life.

13. Rhinoceros hornbills have long wings and a long tail. These make them strong fliers.

14. These birds live in the tops of the trees in Southeast Asia.

15. They can live up to 35 years.

16. The rhinoceros hornbill is the national bird of Malaysia.

1. This insect got its name because the horn on its head looks like a rhinoceros's horn.

2. The rhinoceros beetle is super strong.

3. This beetle can lift 30 times its own weight and still run. That would be like a human carrying a full-grown … well, rhinoceros.

4. Some adult beetles can even lift 100 times their weight, but they can't move at that point.

5. Males use their strength to fight other males.

6. In some countries, people bet on which of these beetles can win a fight.

7. Rhinoceros beetles are found on every continent except Antarctica.

8. They are one of the largest species of beetle.

9. A rhinoceros beetle is about 6 inches (15 cm) long.

10. Rhinoceros beetles eat nectar, sap, and fruit.

11. Beetle larvae eat decaying plants. Yum!

12. Female beetles lay about 50 eggs.

13. Rhinoceros beetles only live for a year or two.

14. Much of that time is spent as larvae.

15. When a rhinoceros beetle feels threatened, it rubs its wings against its abdomen to make a squeaking noise.

16. Some people keep rhinoceros beetles as pets.

RHINOCEROS BEETLE

RHEA

1. These big birds have long wings, but they cannot fly.

2. Instead, they use their wings to keep their balance as they run.

3. Rheas are fast runners and can reach speeds of up to 40 miles (64 km) an hour.

4. They are the largest bird in South America.

5. A rhea weighs between 33 and 66 pounds (15 and 30 kg).

6. It is 3 to 5 feet (0.9 to 1.5 meters) tall.

7. Rheas usually live in groups.

8. Males live by themselves during breeding season.

9. A rhea will eat just about anything, including plants, seeds, fruit, insects, small birds, frogs, and lizards.

10. A rhea has three toes on each foot.

11. Males attract females by making a booming noise and flapping their wings.

12. They may mate with up to 12 females.

13. After they mate, the male digs a nest in the ground.

14. Each female lays up to five gold-colored eggs in the nest.

15. The male sits on the nest until the eggs hatch about six weeks later.

16. He takes care of all the chicks and chases away any animal that comes near.

PURPLE FROG

1. This creature is also called the pignose frog.

2. It only lives in one place in the world— the Western Ghat mountains in India.

3. It was not known or written about by scientists until 2003.

4. Purple frogs look like turtles without a shell.

5. They live underground for most of the year.

6. Purple frogs only come to the surface for two to three weeks during monsoon season.

7. During this time, they mate, and females lay eggs in the water.

8. These frogs are only about 2.75 inches (7 cm) long.

9. They have strong front legs, which help them dig their burrows.

10. But they can't hop because their back legs are too short.

11. Instead of hopping, the purple frog runs.

12. These frogs use their great sense of smell to find termites to eat.

13. There are only about 135 of these blobby creatures left in the wild.

14. Only a few of the remaining frogs are female.

PUFFERFISH

1. These fish really know how to scare away predators.

2. When they are threatened, they blow up their bodies by sucking in lots of water and air.

3. Some species also have pointy spikes all over their bodies.

4. Pufferfish also contain a toxic substance.

5. That toxin tastes really bad and can even kill any animal that tries to eat the fish.

6. Pufferfish poison can also kill a human.

7. One pufferfish has enough poison to kill 30 people.

8. More bad news—there is no antidote to pufferfish poison.

9. In Japan, this fish is considered good to eat, but chefs have to be specially trained to prepare it safely.

10. There are more than 190 species of pufferfish.

11. Pufferfish live in oceans all over the world.

12. Some live in fresh water too.

13. They eat algae and small invertebrates.

14. A large pufferfish can crack open and eat a clam.

15. The smallest pufferfish is just 1 inch (2.5 cm) long.

16. The largest is the Mbu pufferfish, which can grow more than 2 feet (0.6 meter) long.

17. Pufferfish have two upper teeth and two lower teeth.

18. The teeth are fused together to form a hard beak.

19. Pufferfish chew on hard substances to file down their teeth and keep them healthy.

20. Pufferfish have great eyesight.

21. They can move each eye independently, which helps them find their prey and spot predators.

22. They are the only bony fish that can close their eyes.

23. But pufferfish don't have eyelids!

24. Instead, they pull their eyeballs into their sockets and suck the skin around them closed.

25. Pufferfish can change color.

26. Some male pufferfish make beautiful nests in the sand.

27. These nests have geometric patterns and can be 6.5 feet (2 meters) wide.

28. They even decorate the nests with shells to make them look pretty.

29. Baby pufferfish are cannibals and will take bites out of their brothers and sisters.

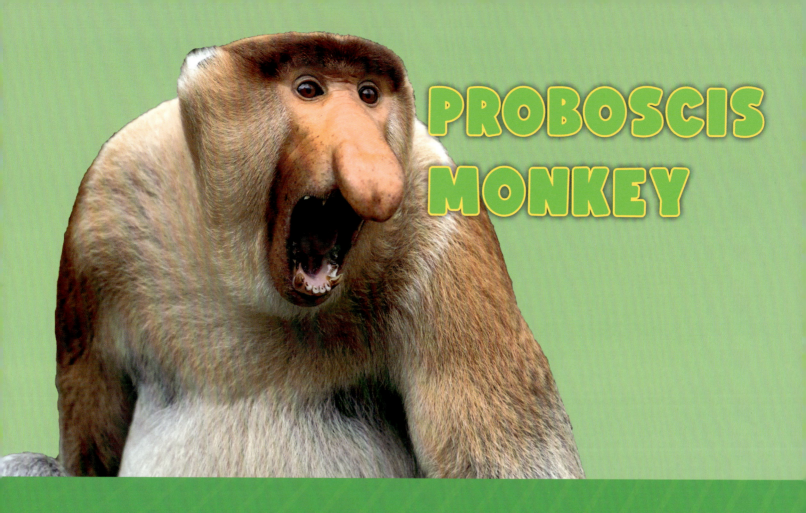

PROBOSCIS MONKEY

1. "Proboscis" is another word for nose, and this monkey sure has a big one.

2. That big nose helps amplify the sound when a male monkey is calling for a mate.

3. Males open their mouth wide and stick out their teeth, then make a deep growling noise.

4. The proboscis monkey has the largest nose of any primate.

5. Proboscis monkeys live in large family groups.

6. Females care for their own babies and help care for other babies in the group too.

7. Proboscis monkeys eat tough mangrove leaves.

8. These leaves are hard to digest, but the monkey's big stomach is full of bacteria that does the job.

9. Proboscis monkeys are good swimmers.

10. Sometimes they will jump into the water with a big belly flop.

11. They are also great at swinging from tree to tree with their long arms.

12. Females are much smaller than males, and their noses are a lot smaller too.

13. These monkeys only live in jungles on the islands in Borneo.

14. It is illegal to kill or capture these creatures.

PRAYING MANTIS

1. These insects got their name from the way they hold their front legs. It looks like the creature is saying its prayers.

2. Insects that get too close to a praying mantis might want to say their prayers, because the mantis is a fierce hunter.

3. The praying mantis grabs its prey with those long front legs.

4. Those legs are covered with sharp spines to hold on to the prey.

5. It eats crickets, spiders, frogs, lizards, and even small birds.

6. A praying mantis usually eats its prey head first.

7. Many gardeners like having praying mantises around because they eat harmful insects.

8. You can find praying mantises in warm places in North and South America, Europe, Asia, and Africa.

9. A praying mantis can turn its head 180 degrees, or half a circle.

10. These insects have excellent vision.

11. They are also great at jumping.

12. A praying mantis's green and brown coloring helps it hide among leaves and branches.

13. Females often bite off the male's head after mating with him.

PORCUPINE

1. Porcupines are the second-largest rodent in North America.

2. Only the beaver is bigger.

3. Porcupines are covered with sharp quills that are about 2 to 3 inches (5 to 7 cm) long.

4. These quills are hollow.

5. The quills are loosely attached to the porcupine's fur, which makes it easy for this creature to shake them onto any predator that gets too close.

6. Many people believe porcupines shoot their quills, but this is not true.

7. A single porcupine has about 30,000 quills.

8. Porcupines spend most of their time on the ground, looking for plants to eat.

9. Porcupines are also great at climbing trees, thanks to rough skin on their feet that gives them a good grip.

10. They are good swimmers too.

11. A baby porcupine is called a porcupette.

12. Females usually have just one porcupette at a time.

13. A porcupette has soft quills when it is born.

14. Porcupines live in forests all over North America.

POISON DART FROG

1. These frogs' bright colors don't just make them look pretty. They are a powerful warning.

2. Poison dart frogs are one of the most poisonous creatures on Earth.

3. The golden poison dart frog has enough poison to kill 20,000 mice—or 20 humans.

4. Scientists think the frog's body makes poison out of chemicals in some of the insects they eat in the wild.

5. Frogs kept in captivity and fed a different diet are not poisonous.

6. These frogs got their name because Indigenous people once placed their poison on the tips of darts they used for hunting.

7. A poison dart frog catches its prey by slurping it up with its long, sticky tongue.

8. Although most frogs are good swimmers, this species is not.

9. Also unlike most other frogs, poison dart frogs are active during the day.

10. Poison dart frogs like it hot! They live in tropical forests in Central and South America.

11. These frogs spend most of the time on the ground, but they can also climb trees.

12. They can be very noisy as they call to one another in the forest.

13. Loss of habitat has endangered many species of poison dart frog.

14. Many are also illegally sold as pets.

PLATYPUS

1. This animal is so weird looking that when people in Europe first saw it, they thought the creature was a hoax.

2. A British scientist named George Shaw received a platypus specimen in the 1790s. He thought it was several animals stitched together.

3. He didn't believe the platypus was real until he took the specimen apart.

4. Platypuses are only found in Australia.

5. A platypus has a tail like a beaver, a bill like a bird, webbed feet like a duck, and a body like an otter. No wonder people thought it was fake!

6. This animal can store fat in its tail.

7. A male platypus has hollow spurs on its back legs.

8. These spurs are connected to a gland filled with venom.

9. Scientists think platypuses use these venom-filled spurs when they are fighting.

10. Platypuses wrap their legs around their victim and push the spurs into the other animal's body.

11. The venom isn't strong enough to kill, but it causes swelling and extreme pain.

12. The platypus is one of just a few mammals that lay eggs.

13. After she lays one to three eggs, the female tucks them between her bottom and her tail to keep them warm.

14. The eggs hatch in about ten days.

15. Babies are called puggles. Aww!

16. Each puggle is only as big as a bean.

17. Puggles stay with them mother in a burrow for three or four months.

18. The platypus's thick fur helps it stay warm underwater.

19. Although this animal's fur looks brown, it glows green and blue under ultraviolet light. No one is sure why.

20. Platypuses walk on their knuckles to protect the webbing on their feet.

21. Their webs are actually extra pieces of skin that fold back when the platypus is on land.

22. A platypus's bill has thousands of sensory receptors.

23. These receptors help the animal find its way underwater.

24. They also help the platypus find the shrimp it likes to eat.

25. A platypus has no teeth.

26. Instead, it has bony plates in its mouth to grind up food.

27. When it is underwater, a platypus closes its ears, eyes, and nose to keep water out.

28. Platypuses live in lakes, ponds, and streams.

29. They spend 10 to 12 hours a night in the water.

30. During the day, they hang out in burrows along the shore.

31. A platypus can survive in many different habitats.

PIRANHA

1. The name "piranha" means "tooth fish" in the native Tupi language of Brazil.

2. These fish are only 8 to 12 inches (20 to 30.5 cm) long. But they have a fearsome reputation!

3. A piranha's mouth is filled with lots of razor-sharp teeth.

4. This fish can replace its teeth if they break or fall out.

5. Many people believe a school of piranha can kill a large animal.

6. Actually, piranhas usually eat plants, fish, crabs, shrimp, and small animals.

7. If they are really hungry, they sometimes eat each other.

8. There are only a few reports of them attacking people.

9. They live in South American rivers.

10. Herons, crocodiles, and river dolphins prey on piranhas.

11. These fish can make barking or grunting sounds.

12. They make these noises by expelling air from an organ called the swim bladder.

13. Some people keep piranhas as pets.

PILL BUG

1. Pill bugs are not bugs. They aren't even insects.

2. They are actually crustaceans and are closely related to shrimp and crayfish.

3. Pill bugs are the only crustaceans that live on land.

4. They are also called roly-polys.

5. They are covered with a hard exoskeleton.

6. When a pill bug is threatened, it rolls its body into a ball. • • • • • • • • • • • • • • • • •

7. These creatures live in humid environments.

8. They eat rotting plant matter.

9. Even though it lives on land, a pill bug breathes through gills.

10. A female pill bug carries its eggs around in a pouch.

11. Pill bugs don't pee.

12. Instead, they pass waste material out through their exoskeleton.

13. A pill bug drinks water through its mouth, but also through its butt!

14. They have blue blood and eat their own poop.

PEACOCK FLOUNDER

1. This fish is almost totally flat.

2. Its shape helps it hide in the sandy bottom of the ocean.

3. Peacock flounder are also called plate fish because of their flat shape.

4. When this fish is born, it has an eye on each side of its head.

5. Over time, the right eye moves to the left side of its body, so both eyes are on the same side.

6. A peacock flounder can change colors to match its surroundings.

7. This fish lives near coral reefs in the western Atlantic Ocean.

8. It also lives near mangroves and seagrass.

9. The peacock flounder lies still, waiting for prey to come close enough for it to grab.

10. This fish eats small fish, crustaceans, and small octopuses.

1. It's easy to tell male and female peacocks apart.

2. Females are usually gray, brown, or white.

3. Males are bright blue and green.

4. Males and females look alike when they are born.

5. Males start to develop their bright colors when they are about three months old.

6. Males spread their tails to attract a mate.

7. The spots on a peacock's tail are called eyespots or ocellus.

8. Peacocks are native to India.

9. They are a symbol of Indian royalty and the national bird of India.

10. Although their tails are heavy, peacocks can fly.

11. They hang out on tree branches to nest or escape predators.

12. These birds can make very loud squawks and hoots.

13. They live between 10 and 25 years.

PEACOCK

ODDBALL
FAST FACTS!
10 SUPER-SMART ANIMALS

1. Squirrels can remember where they buried seeds and nuts for the winter. These rodents can even trick other animals by pretending to bury food in one spot, while actually hiding it somewhere else.

2. Raccoons can figure out puzzles and traps. They often get into the most secure garbage cans to find food. Their long fingers and clever brains make it possible for these animals to pick locks and open even the trickiest latches.

3. Rats have excellent memories. They can learn patterns and remember them, which is a big sign of intelligence. This skill makes it easy for rats to figure out a maze.

4. Crows are so smart, they know how to use tools. They bend sticks into hooks to catch insects. Crows have even been spotted watching out for cars, then dropping nuts on the road in time for the cars to crack them as they drive over them. These birds are also able to remember places and faces. No birdbrains here!

5. Pigs are great communicators. Along with sounds, they "talk" to each other by touching each other with their mouths. They can also solve problems and have a great memory. Weird fact: Scientists have trained some pigs to use joysticks to play video games!

6. An octopus has the largest brain of any invertebrate. Scientists have counted more than half a billion neurons, or nerve cells, in an octopus's brain.

7. Have you heard the saying, "An elephant never forgets"? It might be true! Elephants have great memories. They can remember who's who and recognize elephants that don't belong to their herd. Elephants can also remember good places to find food and water. They can even remember an old friend that they haven't seen in a while.

8. Orangutans are part of a group called primates, which also includes apes and monkeys. All of these animals are very smart, and the orangutan is one of the smartest. These animals can use tools and solve problems. Some have even learned sign language to communicate with people.

9. Chimpanzees are another member of the primate family. These creatures have a complex society with close relationships among family members. They use tools, can learn sign language, and solve puzzles.

10. Dolphins may be the smartest animals on Earth. They have a complex language that people don't understand, but other dolphins do. These mammals have super-sized brains. They use tools and like to play, both of which are signs they are super-smart.

PANGOLIN

1. This creature looks like it is walking around in a suit of armor.

2. It is actually covered in scales made of keratin.

3. They are the only mammal with scales.

4. When it feels threatened, a pangolin will curl up into a ball.

5. It's impossible for a predator to bite through its tough scales.

6. A pangolin can also release a stinky spray from a gland under its tail.

7. Pangolins live in Asia and Africa.

8. They eat ants and termites.

9. They dig up these insects with their long, strong claws.

10. Then the animal slurps up its prey with its long tongue.

11. A pangolin's tongue can be longer than its body.

12. One pangolin can eat up to 70 million insects a year.

13. They close their ears and nostrils while they are eating. No one wants a termite crawling into its ears!

14. Pangolins are the most trafficked animal in the world.

15. People kill pangolins for their scales and meat.

OSTRICH

1. The ostrich is the largest bird in the world.

2. Male ostriches stand up to 9 feet (3 meters) tall.

3. They weigh between 220 and 287 pounds (99 to 130 kg).

4. Females are a bit smaller, but still huge.

5. Ostriches have wings, but these birds are too heavy to fly.

6. Instead, they run across the grasslands of Africa, where they live.

7. An ostrich can run as fast as 43 miles (70 km) an hour.

8. It can cover up to 16 feet (5 meters) in one stride.

9. An ostrich has two long claws on each foot.

10. A kick from an ostrich can kill a lion.

11. If an ostrich doesn't want to fight, it will lie flat on the ground to hide from danger.

12. Its black and brown feathers help camouflage it on the ground.

13. These birds mostly eat seeds, grass, and fruit.

14. Sometimes they eat insects and lizards as well.

15. Ostriches live in big groups called herds.

16. Ostrich eggs are the largest in the world.

17. Males attract females by dancing.

OPOSSUM

1. Opossums are the only marsupials that live in North America.

2. All other marsupials live in Australia.

3. Females give birth to up to 25 babies.

4. The babies are hairless and blind, and only about the size of a honeybee.

5. They crawl into a pouch on their mother's stomach.

6. There are only 13 nipples in the pouch for the babies to nurse from, so the last ones to crawl in have no chance to survive.

7. Babies stay in the pouch for 50 to 70 days.

8. When they are big enough to come out, they ride on their mother's back.

9. About four months later, the babies are all grown up and ready to go out on their own.

10. Opossums have a prehensile tail.

11. They use their tail to hang from tree branches.

12. An opossum's tail is hairless, which means it can get frostbitten in the winter.

13. Opossums eat just about anything.

14. Earthworms, insects, plants, even garbage all taste good to an opossum.

15. When an opossum is threatened, it plays dead—meaning it actually passes out.

16. It bares its teeth in a death grimace.

17. It has no control over pretending to be dead.

18. An opossum can "play dead" for up to six hours.

19. The opossum will also give off a nasty smell from its butt.

20. Most predators think the opossum is dead and decaying and stay away.

21. Opossums are usually nocturnal.

22. Sometimes they come out during the day, especially in cold weather.

23. Opossums don't hibernate, but they often hang out in an underground den during the winter.

24. Opossums are immune to snake venom.

25. Unlike most mammals, opossums rarely get rabies.

26. An opossum has an opposable thumb on each back foot.

27. This thumb is called a hallux.

28. The hallux helps the opossum climb trees and hold things.

OKAPI

1. This animal looks like a cross between a zebra and a deer.

2. They are related to giraffes (but are much shorter!).

3. An okapi's stripes help it hide in the forest.

4. The stripes look like sun shining through the trees.

5. Okapis only live in the rain forests in one part of Africa.

6. Its thick, oily fur helps it stay dry in the rain.

7. An okapi has scent glands on the bottom of its hooves.

8. These glands mark the animal's territory.

9. An okapi's short horns are covered with skin.

10. Females have small bumps instead of horns.

11. Okapis eat many types of plants.

12. They have four stomachs to help digest tough plant material.

13. An okapi has a long, dark tongue.

14. It uses its tongue to strip leaves from trees.

15. An okapi can eat up to 60 pounds (27 kg) of food a day.

16. It also sometimes eats bat poop and clay. These provide important minerals.

17. An okapi calf can stand up just 30 minutes after it is born.

18. Calves don't poop for the first month, so that the smell doesn't attract predators.

19. Mama okapis will beat the ground with their hooves to scare away predators.

OCTOPUS

1. An octopus has eight arms.

2. The bottom of each arm is covered with suction cups.

3. Two-third of an octopus's neurons, or nerve endings, are in its arms.

4. An octopus uses its arms to grab food.

5. The tentacles can taste and touch at the same time.

6. An octopus has three hearts.

7. Its blood is blue.

8. An octopus has no skeleton or shell.

9. Its soft body is able to squeeze through small holes.

10. In 2016, an octopus escaped from its tank in a New Zealand aquarium, squeezed through a drain, and swam out to sea.

11. Octopuses are very smart.

12. They have been known to escape from their tanks, eat animals in other tanks, then go back to their own tank.

13. The only hard part of an octopus's body is its powerful beak.

14. Its beak and jaws are on the underside of its body.

15. Octopus species range in size from less than 1 inch (0.5 cm) to more than 16 feet (5 meters) long.

NUDIBRANCH

1. Nudibranchs are also called sea slugs.
2. They are part of the mollusk family.
3. They live in oceans all over the world.
4. A nudibranch has a shell when it is a larvae.
5. The shell breaks off when the nudibranch is an adult.
6. Nudibranchs come in many bright colors and more than 3,000 species.
7. There are two main types of nudibranch.
8. One type breathes through soft spikes on its body.
9. The other absorbs oxygen through gills around its butt.
10. The "horns" on a nudibranch's head are actually nostrils.
11. They are called rhinophores.
12. Rhinophores are great at picking up smells in the water, which helps the nudibranch find food.
13. Nudibranchs are carnivores. They eat anemones, coral, sponges, and even other nudibranchs.
14. Nudibranchs get their bright colors from the coral and anemones they eat.
15. Some species have a tooth-covered tongue they use to scrape food from rocks.
16. Others suck food into their bodies.
17. Nudibranchs mate by lying next to each other and connecting their reproductive organs.
18. Sometimes those organs break off, but they grow back.

NARWHAL

1. These creatures are sometimes called the "unicorn of the sea."

2. Most male narwhals have a long tusk sticking out of their head.

3. The tusk is actually a really long tooth.

4. It has more than 10 million nerve endings inside.

5. A tusk can grow up to 8.5 feet (2.6 meters) long.

6. Babies are born without tusks.

7. Narwhals live in the chilly Arctic Ocean.

8. They eat many kinds of fish, squid, and shrimp.

9. A narwhal can dive up to a mile (1.6 km) deep to find food.

10. They change color as they age, going from blue-gray to gray to white.

11. Narwhals live in social groups called pods.

1. These animals aren't really naked. They do have some hair on their bodies.

2. A naked mole rat can move its teeth independently, like chopsticks.

3. Mole rats live underground.

4. They build complex underground tunnels and rooms.

5. Some rooms are used for eating, others for nesting, and some for going to the bathroom.

6. A tunnel can be up to 2.5 miles (4 km) long.

7. Naked mole rats live in large groups.

8. Some of the mole rats serve as soldiers.

9. Soldiers block the tunnel entrance with their bodies to keep predators out.

10. A naked mole rat's biggest enemy is a snake.

11. These animals are almost blind, but they have a great sense of smell.

12. They communicate by making 17 different sounds, including hisses and chirps.

13. A mole rat baby weighs less than a penny.

14. Most rodents only live for a few years, but naked mole rats can live into their thirties.

15. These creatures have powerful claws for digging underground.

16. They eat the underground parts of plants.

17. Naked mole rats get all the water they need from their food.

18. They live in the eastern parts of Africa.

NAKED MOLE RAT

MUDSKIPPER

1. The mudskipper is a real fish out of water.

2. This fish can skip, climb, and even walk on land.

3. Its front fins are shaped like legs, which helps them move on land.

4. Their eyes move independently, which helps them see on both land and water.

5. Mudskippers live in swamps and lagoons.

6. They spend most of their time sitting on tree roots and rocks.

7. When they are on land, mudskippers rub water over their gills so they can breathe.

8. These creatures can also breathe through their skin.

9. Mudskippers dig underwater burrows by scooping out mud with their mouths.

10. They keep an air bubble inside their burrow so they can breathe.

11. Mudskippers eat insects, worms, and small crustaceans.

MIMIC OCTOPUS

1. This creature is a master of disguise.

2. The mimic octopus got its name because it can mimic, or copy, other species.

3. The mimic octopus can change color to mimic other animals that are venomous.

4. This trick fools predators into staying away.

5. A mimic octopus has tiny pigment sacs all over its body that can change into different colors.

6. They also mimic the movements of other animals, like fish or sea snakes.

7. This creature usually buries itself in the sand at the bottom of the ocean or river and waits for prey to swim past.

8. Scientists didn't discover this octopus until 1998.

9. These octopuses only live for about nine months.

10. Baby octopuses take care of themselves—and learn to mimic—as soon as they're born.

1. These animals aren't shrimp, but they are related to them.

2. They are part of a group called stomatopod crustaceans.

3. They got the name "mantis" because they fold their front legs like a praying mantis does.

4. Mantis shrimp come in many bright colors and patterns and in over 450 species.

5. Scientists divide mantis shrimp into two groups.

6. Spearing mantis shrimp kill their prey by impaling their prey on their sharp front legs.

7. Smashing mantis shrimp use their club-shaped tail to smash their prey to death.

8. A blow from a smashing mantis's tail can break aquarium glass.

9. A mantis shrimp's eyes are found at the end of long stalks.

10. These eyes can move independently, which gives this creature fantastic vision.

11. They've been on Earth longer than the dinosaurs.

MANTIS SHRIMP

MANATEE

1. Manatees are also called sea cows.

2. They are related to elephants.

3. Manatees live in bays and coastal waters.

4. Unlike most marine mammals, they can live in both fresh and salt water.

5. Manatees are big animals. Adults are up to 13 feet (4 meters) long and weigh up to 3,500 pounds (1588 kg).

6. Manatees are about 4 feet (1.2 meters) long when they are born.

7. Newborns weigh between 60 and 70 pounds (27 to 32 kg).

8. They have heavy bones.

9. Manatees only eat plants.

10. The seagrass that grows at the bottom of the water is their favorite food.

11. A manatee's weight helps it sink to the bottom of the water to feed.

12. They use their heavy tail to steer through the water.

13. A manatee can hold its breath for up to 20 minutes.

14. Manatees often have algae growing on their bodies.

15. Barnacles often grow on a manatee's skin as well.

16. A manatee's teeth regrow throughout its life.

17. There are three species of manatee.

18. One species lives along the Florida coast.

19. The other two species live in the Amazon River and the coast of Africa.

20. Manatees are born underwater.

21. Their mothers push them to the surface so they can take their first breath.

22. After just an hour, the baby can swim and surface on its own.

23. Manatees are the origin of the mermaid story. Sailors who spotted these creatures thought they were humans with tails.

24. Christopher Columbus wrote the first description of a manatee in 1492.

25. If it's lucky, a manatee can live up to 60 years.

26. Manatees are in danger.

27. Some are hunted for their skins, oil, and bones.

28. Others are hit and killed by motorboats or caught in fishing nets.

ODDBALL

FAST FACTS!

12 SURPRISING ANIMAL FRIENDSHIPS

1. **Water Buffalo and Cattle Egrets:** The birds eat insects on the water buffalo's skin, or insects that are kicked up by the buffalo's feet.

2. **Egyptian Crocodiles and Plovers:** You would think that a crocodile would make a quick lunch of a bird pecking in its mouth, but no! The bird eats leftover food, and the crocodile doesn't mind because the bird keeps its teeth clean and healthy.

3. **Ostriches and Zebras:** Ostriches and zebras work together to spot predators in time to run away. Ostriches use their sense of smell, while zebras use their excellent eyesight.

4. **Colombian Lesserback Tarantulas and Humming Frogs:** These animals often nest together. The spiders protect the frog, while the frog eats insects that might otherwise chow down on the spider's eggs.

5. **Honeyguides and Honey Badgers:** Honeyguides are birds that love honey, but they aren't strong enough to break open a beehive. Instead, they hang out with honey badgers and share the meal when the honey badger rips open a beehive with its sharp claws.

6. **Clownfish and Sea Anemones:** Anemones are poisonous, but the clownfish is immune to their toxins. The clownfish has safe shelter hiding inside the anemones, and it chases away predators that might harm the anemone.

7. **Coyotes and Badgers:** These two animals often hunt together. The badger can dig up prey underground, and then the two buddies share a meal.

8. **Drongos and Meerkats:** These birds follow meerkats as they hunt and sound an alarm call if a predator comes near. The meerkat often drops its prey as it runs away, leaving it behind for the drongo to eat.

9. **Pistol Shrimp and Gobies:** Pistol shrimp are fierce predators, but they have terrible eyesight. The goby uses its great vision to spot predators. In return, the shrimp lets the fish live in its burrow.

....

10. **Aphids and Ants:** Ants "milk" aphids to get a sweet liquid called honeydew. Ants even raise aphids the way people raise farm animals. What does the aphid get out of this? The ants protect the aphids from predators and parasites.

....

11. **Oxpeckers and Rhinos:** These little birds like to pick insects off the backs of their rhino buddies. In return, they will alert the rhino if danger comes near. Oxpeckers also hang around wildebeest, zebras, and other large grazing animals.

....

12. **Sharks and Remoras:** Sharks are fierce predators, but they don't bother the remora rays swimming alongside them. That's because the remoras eat parasites that nest in the shark's cartilage. The shark protects its friends because who would want to challenge a shark?

....

1. Lobsters come in different colors, but greenish-brown is the most common.

2. Other colors come from a genetic mutation.

3. Lobsters turn red when they are cooked because the red pigment is the only one that can stand the heat.

4. Albino lobsters are white and do not turn red when cooked.

5. Lobsters have two front claws.

6. One claw is much bigger than the other and is used for crushing prey.

7. That claw has a ridged edge that is used to break open clams and crabs.

8. The other claw is used for grabbing soft prey, like worms or fish.

9. The crusher claw is always on the lobster's dominant side.

LOBSTER

10. Lobsters also have eight legs that they use for walking.

11. Lobsters have clear blood.

12. Lobsters "smell" with their legs.

13. They have sensory hairs on their legs that help them find food.

14. These hairs also allow the lobster to taste its food.

15. If a lobster loses a claw or leg, it can grow a new one.

16. However, it takes about five years for the new claw or leg to be as big as the previous one.

17. Lobsters have no teeth.

18. Instead, an organ called a gastric mill grinds up food before passing it into the lobster's stomach.

19. A lobster's stomach is located behind its eyes.

20. Lobsters grow by molting. This means they shed their shells and grow new ones.

21. Lobsters are vulnerable to predators while they are molting.

22. A lobster molts about 25 times during its life.

23. It often eats its old shell because it provides a lot of calcium.

24. They never stop growing and may live for up to 100 years.

25. Lobsters can swim backward.

26. A lobster's brain is missing the part that senses pain in other animals, so many scientists think lobsters don't feel pain.

27. The largest lobster ever caught was 3.5 feet (over 1 meter) long and weighed more than 44 pounds (20 kg).

6

1. Little brown bats live all over North America.

2. They eat moths, mosquitoes, and other insects.

3. Bats find their prey using echolocation.

4. They make high-pitched squeaks that bounce off objects around them, letting the bat sense what is there.

5. A bat has to eat at least half its body weight in insects each night to survive.

6. Bats are nocturnal, so they are most active just after dusk.

7. Bats roost in large groups called colonies.

8. They roost in caves, hollow trees, and inside buildings.

9. Bats hang upside-down when they are sleeping.

10. A female has one baby, or pup, a year.

11. She can identify her pup by smell and sound.

12. Pups stay with their mom for about a month. By then, they can fly and catch their own food.

13. Bats hibernate during the winter.

14. A disease called white-nose syndrome has killed many bats.

15. White-nose syndrome makes bats wake up during hibernation, and they die because they use up all their energy trying to keep warm.

LITTLE BROWN BAT

LIONFISH

1. These fish are very dramatic looking.

2. Their bodies are covered with long fins and spines.

3. The spines are attached to venom sacs along the fish's backbone.

4. A lionfish's sting causes extreme pain, trouble breathing, and paralysis.

5. A lionfish can grow to be up to 18 inches (46 cm) long.

6. But baby lionfish are less than 1 inch (2.5 cm) long.

7. A lionfish is carnivorous. It eats other fish, shrimp, and crabs.

8. Lionfish corner their prey with their long fins, then swallow them whole.

9. Lionfish once lived only in the Pacific and Indian Oceans.

10. However, they have invaded the Atlantic Ocean as well.

11. Scientists are concerned about this invasion because lionfish can kill off native fish.

12. Lionfish have no known predators.

13. Females can release up to two million eggs each year.

14. Some people keep lionfish as pets.

LIGHTNING BUG

1. These insects are also called fireflies.

2. They get their name because they can light up.

3. A firefly has two chemicals in its tail.

4. These chemicals combine to create light.

5. A lightning bug produces "cold light." Its energy creates light that doesn't make heat.

6. These insects use light to communicate with each other.

7. Each species flashes its own specific light pattern.

8. Some lightning bug eggs and larvae glow too.

9. Lightning bugs live for one to two years.

10. They spend most of that time in the larval stage.

11. Adult lightning bugs only live long enough to mate and lay eggs. They do not even eat.

12. Many animals don't eat lightning bugs because these insects give off a chemical that tastes bad.

LEAFY SEA DRAGON

1. This fish is related to seahorses.

2. It lives in coral reefs off the coast of Australia.

3. Its fins look like leaves and strands of seaweed.

4. Those fins make it easy for the fish to hide in kelp beds.

5. Leafy sea dragons can also change color to blend in.

6. Leafy sea dragons eat tiny creatures called mysids.

7. They wait until the mysids get close, then suck them in through their straw-like mouth.

8. A leafy sea dragon has no stomach.

9. This fish can slurp up thousands of mysids a day.

10. A female leafy sea dragon lays up to 300 eggs.

11. After a female lays eggs, the male carries them around on the underside of his tail.

12. The babies hatch about four weeks later and can take care of themselves right away.

13. A baby leafy sea dragon is only about 0.8 inch (20 mm) long.

14. These fish are rare and are protected by the Australian government.

LEAF INSECT

1. Leaf insects are masters of camouflage.

2. They look just like, well, a leaf!

3. Females have wings but cannot fly.

4. Leaf insects eat berries and leaves.

5. These insects are quiet during the day and active at night.

6. They walk in a stop-and-go motion, like a leaf blowing in the wind.

7. Young leaf bugs are called nymphs.

8. Nymphs are reddish-brown. They turn green after they grow up and start eating leaves.

9. There are about 50 different species of leaf insect.

10. They live in warm places in Asia and Australia.

11. Some species have bumps on their antennae that make sounds when they are rubbed together.

1. This bird might be little, but it makes a big noise!

2. They make a loud noise when they are defending their territory.

3. These birds are loudest at dawn and dusk.

4. The laughing kookaburra's call was used to create jungle sounds in old Tarzan movies.

5. Laughing kookaburras are the largest member of the kingfisher family.

6. These birds live in Australia.

7. They eat insects, amphibians, small reptiles, and crabs.

8. Laughing kookaburras mate for life.

9. A female lays two or three eggs.

10. Chicks have hooks on their beaks.

11. Often, two chicks will peck a third chick to death so they can have more food.

12. Young kookaburras often stay with their parents and help raise new chicks.

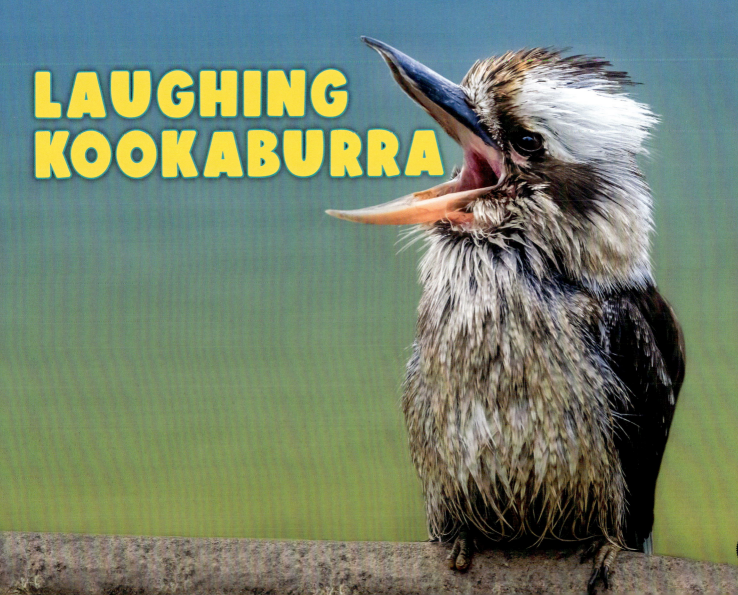

LAUGHING KOOKABURRA

ODDBALL

FAST FACTS!

10 OUTRAGEOUS ANIMAL APPETITES

1. **Pygmy Shrew:** This animal may be small, but its metabolism is super-sized. Its heart beats up to 1,000 beats a minute when it's resting and even faster when it moves around. To stay alive, a pygmy shrew eats its weight in food every day. That's an awful lot of insects, spiders, snails, and worms!

2. **Blue Whale:** You can't be the largest animal in the world without needing a lot of food! Oddly enough, these giants of the sea eat teeny-tiny food called krill. It takes about 8,000 pounds (3.5 metric tons) of krill to fill a blue whale's stomach.

3. **Tiger Shark:** These big predators will eat just about anything. Turtles, birds, fish, seals, and other sharks are all on the menu. So is garbage. Scientists have found tires, nails, even car license plates in tiger shark tummies.

4. **Argentine Wide-Mouthed Frog:** This frog's big mouth has given it a cute nickname—the Pac-Man frog! Its mouth is about half the width of its body. When anything comes close, the frog opens up its big mouth and gobbles it up. Argentine wide-mouthed frogs will even try to eat animals bigger than they are.

5. **Python:** This monster snake can swallow an animal bigger than its head. Their prey includes big animals like deer, monkeys, and pigs. They kill their prey by squeezing it to death, then swallowing the animal whole. They may not eat again for weeks.

6. **Caterpillar:** These insects have a lot of work to do. Transforming into a butterfly or moth takes a lot of energy—and food! Caterpillars basically do nothing but eat until it's time for them to change into their next stage of life.

7. Giant Panda: Giant pandas eat one thing and one thing only, and that's bamboo. But this plant does not provide a lot of nutrition. So, a giant panda spends about 14 hours a day eating. They can chow down on 25 to 40 pounds (11 to 18 kg) of bamboo a day. Imagine a huge meal like that on your dinner plate!

8. Elephant: Could you drink 50 gallons (189 liters) of water and eat 350 pounds (159 kg) of food a day? We doubt it! But it takes about 70,000 calories a day for these huge animals to feel full.

9. Tiger: This big cat has a big appetite. It kills large animals and can eat 100 pounds (45 kg) in one meal.

10. Black-Footed Cat: Don't let this kitty's cute appearance fool you! These cats, which live in Canada, can kill and eat an animal every hour. Hunting mostly after dark, they can kill and eat 10 to 14 small mammals or birds a night.

1. Foam grasshoppers get their name from a toxic foam they produce when threatened.

2. The toxins come from the poisonous plants this insect eats.

3. The foam tastes and smells so bad, it scares away any creature that wants to eat it.

4. Its poison is strong enough to kill a dog.

5. This insect's bright colors also warn predators it is bad to eat.

6. Koppies have small front wings and no back wings.

7. They cannot fly.

8. Like other insects, koppies have a hard exoskeleton.

9. As the insect gets bigger, the exoskeleton splits open.

10. The grasshopper sheds its exoskeleton.

11. Then it goes to a safe place to rest while its new exoskeleton hardens.

12. These grasshoppers live in gardens and fields in South Africa.

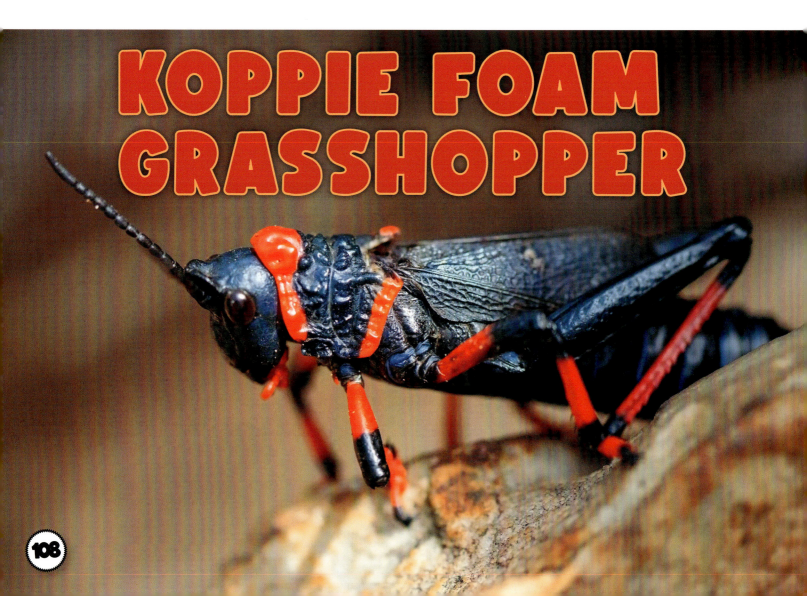

KOPPIE FOAM GRASSHOPPER

KOMODO DRAGON

1. This bad boy is the largest lizard in the world.

2. The Komodo dragon can grow up to 10 feet (3 meters) long and weigh up to 300 pounds (136 kg)!

3. Komodo dragons are very strong.

4. A blow from this creature's tail can kill an animal.

5. A Komodo dragon eats pigs, goats, deer, and other big animals.

6. It bites its prey with its powerful teeth.

7. If the bite doesn't kill its prey, the Komodo dragon just has to wait.

8. The dragon's mouth is full of venom and bacteria that cause its prey's bite wounds to become infected.

9. Once the prey has died from the infection, the Komodo dragon tracks it down using its strong sense of smell.

10. The dragon's jaw can open extra-wide, allowing it to swallow big chunks of meat.

11. It also swallows bones, skin, and hooves. Yummy!

12. A female lays 20 to 40 eggs.

13. Komodo dragons live on islands in Indonesia, where they are protected by the government.

1. This little antelope lives in eastern and southern Africa.

2. It stands just 20 inches (51 cm) tall and weighs between 22 and 40 pounds (10 to 18 kg).

3. Its hooves are only the size of a dime.

4. Those hooves are specially designed to cling to rocks.

5. They're shaped like cylinders and point straight down.

6. A klipspringer can jump onto a spot as small as a sandwich cookie.

7. They can jump 10 to 12 feet (3 to 3.6 meters) into the air.

8. Klipspringers communicate with each other by whistling.

9. They also use poop and chemicals from glands near their eyes to mark their territory.

10. Klipspringers eat fruit, flowers, and plants.

11. These animals mate for life.

12. Mama klipspringers hide their babies behind rocks to keep them safe from predators.

KLIPSPRINGER

KINKAJOU

1. This creature's Latin name means "golden drinker."

2. It uses its long tongue to slurp honey out of beehives.

3. Kinkajous are also called honey bears.

4. Kinkajous also eat fruit, insects, and small mammals.

5. They grab their prey with their sharp front claws.

6. Kinkajous have a long prehensile tail that helps them hang from branches.

7. They can turn their feet backward and run quickly in any direction.

8. Kinkajous are related to raccoons.

9. They live in rainforests in Central and South America.

10. Kinkajous are nocturnal.

11. During the day, they curl up and sleep in holes high in the trees.

12. Kinkajous live in large groups called troops.

13. They like to groom each other.

14. Troop members communicate by loud screeches and barks.

JUMPING SPIDER

1. Some spiders crawl. This spider jumps!

2. These spiders jump on their prey to catch it.

3. The jumping spider changes the blood flow in its body to jump.

4. It contracts its muscles to send more blood to its legs, which sends the spider into the air.

5. A jumping spider can jump up to 50 times its own length.

6. Jumping spiders also dance.

7. Males wave their legs, tap their feet, and bump their abdomens on the ground to get a female's attention.

8. A jumping spider has eight eyes.

9. Four are on the front of its head and four are on the top.

10. Although jumping spiders don't build webs, they do spin silk to make tiny shelters for protection.

11. They also spin a line of silk to anchor themselves when they jump.

12. Jumping spiders are the largest group of spiders on Earth. There are more than 6,200 species.

13. They live almost everywhere in the world, but they like hot, tropical places the best.

1. Jellyfish have been on Earth for more than 600 million years.

2. Scientists have found impressions of jellyfish bodies in ancient fossils.

3. These creatures have no bones.

4. They don't have a brain, lungs, heart, or blood either.

5. A jellyfish is 98 percent water.

6. A jellyfish has receptors that help it sense movement, light, vibrations, and chemicals.

7. They absorb oxygen directly through their skin.

8. Some jellyfish have teeth made of tiny hairs that can rip apart prey.

9. Its mouth is in the center of its body.

10. It uses its mouth to both eat and excrete waste.

11. A jellyfish can also shoot water from its mouth to propel itself through the water.

12. Jellyfish eat tiny zooplankton, crustaceans, and even other jellyfish.

13. Some jellyfish are bioluminescent—they produce their own light.

14. A jellyfish's tentacles are lined with stingers that stun or paralyze its prey.

15. Jellyfish often sting human swimmers too.

JELLYFISH

HUMMINGBIRD

1. Hummingbirds got their name because their wings move so fast, they hum.

2. Hummingbirds are the only birds that can fly backward.

3. They can also hover in place.

4. The smallest bird in the world is the bee hummingbird.

5. The bee hummingbird only lives in Cuba.

6. It is just 2.25 inches (6 cm) long and weighs less than a dime.

7. The bee hummingbird got its name because is so small, it is sometimes mistaken for a bee.

8. Most birds migrate in flocks. But the hummingbird flies alone.

9. Some hummingbirds migrate thousands of miles. That's a long way for such a little bird!

10. A hummingbird can fly 500 miles (805 km) in one trip.

11. Hummingbirds use their long beak to sip sweet nectar from flowers.

12. They flick their tongue up to 18 times a second to lap up the nectar.

13. They can drink twice their body weight in a day.

14. That means visiting up to 1,000 flowers each day.

15. The sugar in nectar gives hummingbirds the energy to survive.

16. Unlike other birds, a hummingbird's body cannot store fat.

17. They have no sense of smell.

18. Instead, they find the flowers they like by color.

19. Red is their favorite color.

20. Hummingbirds also eat insects.

21. They snap them out of the air with their pointed beaks.

22. A hummingbird's legs are so small, they can't walk or hop.

23. Instead, they only use their legs for perching.

24. A female hummingbird usually lays two eggs at a time.

25. Each egg is about the size of a jelly bean.

26. Hummingbirds lay the smallest eggs of any bird.

27. A hummingbird's nest is about the size of a ping-pong ball.

28. They use moss and spiderwebs to line their nests.

29. There are more than 350 species of hummingbirds.

30. All of them live in North or South America.

31. This bird's bright colors gave it the nickname "flying jewels."

1. These flies get their name because they usually live in—You guessed it!—houses.

2. A house fly only lives for 15 to 25 days.

3. These flies can taste with their feet.

4. House flies have no teeth.

5. They can only eat liquids.

6. A house fly will turn a solid food into a liquid by throwing up digestive juices to break it down.

7. Then the fly sips the liquefied food through its tongue.

8. You'll often see house flies on animal poop because of its strong smell.

9. Speaking of poop, scientists think flies poop every time they land.

10. Sticky feet allow the fly to walk upside-down.

11. Flies have compound eyes, which mean they can see in all directions at the same time.

12. They can even see behind them.

13. House flies don't sting or bite, but they are dangerous anyway.

14. Because they hang around garbage and dirty places, these insects can carry and spread more than 100 different kinds of disease-causing germs. Yuck!

HOUSE FLY

HORNED LIZARD

1. These creatures are sometimes called horny toads, but they aren't toads at all.

2. They get their name from the short spikes, or horns, on top of their heads.

3. They eat ants and other insects.

4. Horned lizards catch prey by ambushing it.

5. When an insect gets close, the lizards snags it with its long, sticky tongue.

6. A horned lizard's color helps it blend in with grass and rocks and hide from predators and prey.

7. When it is threatened, a horned lizard will flatten its body.

8. If that doesn't work, the lizard can also swallow air to inflate its body to twice its usual size.

9. The horned lizard has one more scary trick. It can squirt blood from its eyes.

10. It does this by bursting blood vessels around its eyes.

11. The blood also has a nasty taste that makes predators back off.

12. These lizards live in hot deserts in the southwestern United States.

1. Despite its name, this animal is not part of the badger family.

2. Instead, it is related to skunks, otters, and ferrets.

3. It has a HUGE appetite.

4. Honey badgers eat insects, reptiles, birds, amphibians, small mammals, roots, and fruit.

5. They even eat venomous snakes.

6. But their favorite food is honey.

7. Honey badgers love to raid beehives to eat the honey and the larvae.

8. They will also steal food from other animals or scavenge dead animals.

9. Honey badgers have long, sharp claws and teeth.

10. Ripping meat off a bone is no big deal for a honey badger!

11. These animals live in Africa, Asia, Iran, and Saudi Arabia.

12. Some live in cool mountain areas, while others live in hot rainforests.

13. A honey badger has thick, rubbery skin.

14. A honey badger's skin is very loose. If a predator grabs the honey badger, it can twist around and surprise its enemy with a sharp bite.

15. Honey badgers use sticks and rocks as tools.

HONEY BADGER

HOATZIN

1. Hoatzins live in big groups of up to 100 birds.

2. Chicks have claws at the ends of their wings.

3. They use these claws to climb and escape from predators.

4. Hoatzins build their nests over water.

5. If danger is near, the chicks drop into the water to get away.

6. Hoatzins are great swimmers.

7. They have a weird digestive system that ferments the plants they eat. No other bird does this.

8. This process can be smelly, so hoatzins are sometimes called "stink birds."

9. They eat vegetation in swamps and mangroves.

10. These birds are found in South American rainforests.

11. Hoatzins are part of an ancient line of birds.

12. All of its known relatives are extinct.

HERCULES BEETLE

1. This beetle is long, strong, and weird!

2. It lives in the rainforests of Central and South America.

3. It is the longest beetle in the world, measuring up to 6.5 inches (16.5 cm).

4. Males grow huge horns, which they use to fight with each other for mates.

5. They use their horns to lift opponents and throw them to the ground. It's like a wrestling smackdown!

6. The horn can be longer than the rest of the beetle's body.

7. A Hercules beetle's shell, or carapace, can change color depending on the humidity.

8. This beetle can lift up to 100 times its weight.

9. Females lay their eggs in dead trees and logs so the larvae can eat the rotting wood as they grow.

10. They live about three years, but two of those years are spent as larvae.

11. Adult beetles eat rotting fruit they find on the forest floor.

12. They also chew on tree trunks to get the sap inside.

HAIRY FROG

1. This frog has something other amphibians don't—fur! Well, not really.

2. Males grow bristly "hair" on their legs during mating season.

3. The hair is actually thin pieces of skin filled with blood vessels.

4. Scientists think the blood vessels provide extra oxygen to the frog.

5. After the female lays eggs, the male guards them, often staying underwater for several days at a time.

6. Hairy frogs also have crazy claws.

7. They can snap sharp claws out of their toes by breaking their bones and pushing the ends through their skin.

8. The claws are sharp enough to draw blood.

9. After the danger goes away, the frog pulls the bones back into its feet, and the cuts in its skin heal.

10. You can probably tell why this frog is also called the horror frog.

11. It is also called the wolverine frog after the Marvel character who has sharp claws.

HAGFISH

1. Many people think the hagfish is the most disgusting animal on Earth.

2. It is definitely one of the weirdest!

3. The hagfish is sometimes called a slime eel, but it is actually a fish.

4. When it is threatened, a hagfish covers its body with sticky slime made by hundreds of glands along its body.

5. The slime lets the hagfish slide right out of a predator's mouth.

6. To avoid choking on its own slime, the hagfish sneezes the goo out of its nose.

7. Hagfish can also tie themselves into a knot.

8. They move the knot up and down their body to squeeze off the slime.

9. Hagfish have no jaws.

10. Their skull and skeleton are made of cartilage, not bones.

11. It is the only animal that has a skull but no spine.

12. Hagfish also have no stomach or brain.

13. But they do have four hearts.

14. A hagfish has tentacles around its mouth.

15. These tentacles help it sense if food is near.

16. Hagfish often eat the dead bodies of larger animals.

17. They shove their mouth into the dead animal and bore a hole into it with their tooth-covered tongue.

18. Then they eat the animal from the inside out.

19. Eating dead animals might be gross, but it helps keep the ocean clean. So hagfish actually have an important job.

20. They can also absorb nutrients through their skin.

21. Hagfish live in cold waters in oceans all over the world.

22. They burrow into the sand at the bottom of the ocean or hide between rocks to stay safe.

23. Hagfish can go for seven months without eating.

24. Scientists have found a hagfish fossil from 300 million years ago.

25. The fossil looks pretty much the same as hagfish do today.

GREAT FRIGATEBIRD

1. Great frigatebirds are seabirds. But unlike other seabirds, they can't land on the water. Why? Their feathers aren't waterproof.

2. If they did land in the water, their feathers would become so wet and heavy, they would drown.

3. This bird's feet aren't much use either. They are too small to allow the bird to paddle well or even walk.

4. Great frigatebirds eat fish, crustaceans, squid, and jellyfish.

5. This bird's beak is long, thin, and hooked to help it grab fish.

6. These birds are thieves! They often steal food from other birds.

7. A great frigatebird will grab another bird by the tail and shake it violently until the poor bird gives up its food.

8. A male bird has a big, red balloon on its neck.

9. It is called a gular sac.

10. He blows up the sac to attract a mate.

11. It takes about 20 minutes for the sac to inflate with air.

12. Great frigatebirds make a loud drumming sound.

13. These birds are named after large ships called frigates.

14. Like those ships, the birds are fast and maneuver well.

15. This big bird can be up to 3.7 feet (1.1 meter) tall and weigh up to 3.5 pounds (1.5 kg).

16. Their wingspan can be up to 8 feet (2.4 meters).

17. These big birds build big nests! A nest can be about a foot (0.3 meters) wide.

18. Great frigatebirds live in tropical areas. They often fly far over the ocean to feed.

GOBLIN SHARK

1. This shark lives deep in the ocean, where it is always dark.

2. It comes to the surface to feed.

3. The goblin shark has a long snout.

4. Its snout is covered with organs that can sense electricity.

5. This skill helps the shark find prey in the dark.

6. A goblin shark can't fit all of its teeth in its mouth. So, some stick out even when its mouth is closed.

7. This shark can unhinge its jaw when it feeds.

8. Its jaw can stretch out to be as long as its snout.

9. This helps it catch big fish and crustaceans.

10. Baby goblin sharks can take care of themselves as soon as they are born.

1. This insect is not a worm at all. It is actually a beetle.

2. Male glow worms have wings, but females don't.

3. Females glow by emitting a colorful light from their bottoms.

4. The glow attracts males for the females to mate with.

5. Different species have different-colored lights.

6. Glow worm larvae are often found under rocks or in long grass.

7. The larvae feed on slugs and snails that they kill with a toxic bite.

8. The toxins paralyze the slug or snail and eventually dissolve its body.

9. While it is waiting for its prey to dissolve, the larvae often ride around on the snail or slug's back. Yee-haw!

10. Adult glow worms don't eat at all. They don't even have mouth parts.

GLOW WORM

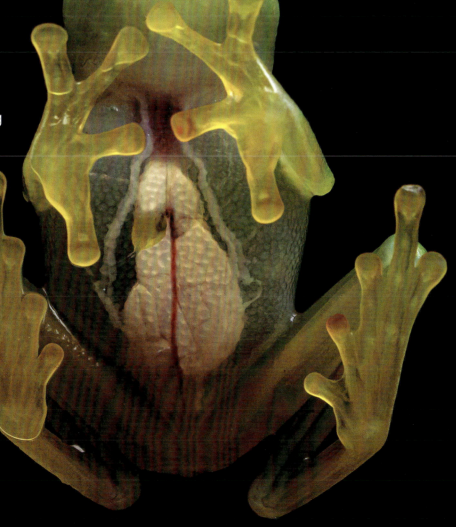

1. These strange frogs get their name because the underside of their bodies are translucent, or see-through, just like glass.

2. You can see this frog's internal organs and even watch its heart beat.

3. Being see-through helps this frog hide in the leaves.

4. Glass frogs live in South and Central America.

5. They spend most of their time in trees.

6. There are about 150 different species of glass frogs.

7. Most frogs lay their eggs in water, but the glass frog lays them on the undersides of leaves hanging over a stream.

8. Male frogs guard the eggs until they hatch.

9. When the eggs hatch, the tadpoles fall into the water below.

10. Unlike other frogs, glass frogs have short tongues.

11. But they are still great at catching prey like ants, spiders, flies, and crickets.

12. Sometimes glass frogs even eat other frogs.

13. These tiny frogs only weigh 0.2 to 0.5 ounce (5.7 to 14 grams).

14. They make a high-pitched whistling sound to attract mates.

GLASS FROG

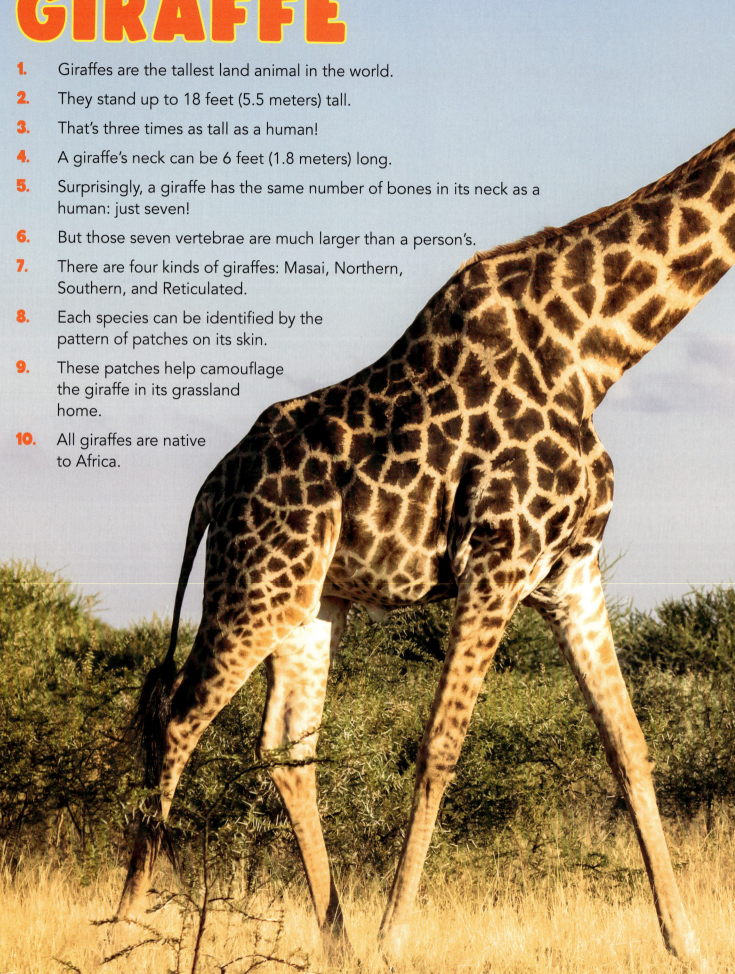

GIRAFFE

1. Giraffes are the tallest land animal in the world.

2. They stand up to 18 feet (5.5 meters) tall.

3. That's three times as tall as a human!

4. A giraffe's neck can be 6 feet (1.8 meters) long.

5. Surprisingly, a giraffe has the same number of bones in its neck as a human: just seven!

6. But those seven vertebrae are much larger than a person's.

7. There are four kinds of giraffes: Masai, Northern, Southern, and Reticulated.

8. Each species can be identified by the pattern of patches on its skin.

9. These patches help camouflage the giraffe in its grassland home.

10. All giraffes are native to Africa.

11. Male giraffes fight by banging their heads and necks together.

12. It looks like a giraffe has horns, but these are ossicones, or cartilage covered with skin.

13. A giraffe's legs can be 6 feet (1.8 meters) long.

14. Those long legs make the animal a fast runner.

15. Giraffes can run up to 34 miles (55 km) an hour.

16. Because they are so tall, giraffes are great at spotting predators like lions.

17. Their height also helps them find food.

18. Giraffes can eat leaves from the tops of trees, which other animals can't reach.

19. A giraffe's tongue is bright blue.

20. That tongue is about 21 inches (53 cm) long.

21. A giraffe's tongue can twist and grip food just like fingers can.

22. A giraffe can eat up to 99 pounds (45 kg) of leaves and twigs a day.

23. Giraffes get most of their water from the plants they eat.

24. That's a good thing, because it's hard for a giraffe to bend all the way down to the ground to drink.

25. Drinking can be dangerous too! Giraffes are in danger from predators when they bend over for a drink.

26. Giraffes give birth standing up.

27. The baby falls about six feet (1.8 meters) to the ground. Ouch!

28. Giraffes only sleep about 30 minutes a day.

29. They take short naps while standing up.

30. A group of giraffes is called a tower.

31. June 21 is World Giraffe Day. That day was chosen because it is usually the longest day of the year.

GILA MONSTER

1. This lizard is covered with pink, orange, and yellow scales that look like beads.

2. Those bright colors warn predators to stay away.

3. That's good advice, because the Gila (pronounced HEE-lah) monster is one of the few poisonous lizards in the world.

4. When a Gila monster bites, venom in glands in its bottom jaws flows into the wound through its grooved teeth.

5. While a Gila monster's bite is very painful, it cannot kill a human.

6. Gila monsters are named after the Gila River Basin in Arizona.

7. That's where they were first discovered.

8. They live in the deserts of the southwestern United States and northwestern Mexico.

9. Gila monsters eat small birds, mammals, lizards, and frogs.

10. They also eat eggs.

11. A Gila monster can eat up to one-third of its body weight in one meal.

12. But it doesn't need to eat very often.

13. It stores extra fat in its tail.

14. Gila monsters spend most of their time in cool underground burrows.

15. They come out only to eat and bask in the sun.

16. Gila monsters spend their whole lives in an area of just 1 square mile (2.6 sq km).

17. Females lay 2 to 12 leathery eggs in an underground nest.

18. When the baby lizards hatch, they can take care of themselves right away.

GIANT WETA

1. This huge grasshopper can be up to 4 inches (10 cm) long.

2. It weighs up to 2.5 ounces (71 grams), or as much as a mouse or small bird.

3. Because it is so heavy, the giant weta cannot fly.

4. It can't even jump.

5. Because it can't fly or jump, wetas are easy prey for rats, reptiles, and birds.

6. Today, these big critters only live on one island in New Zealand.

7. The word "weta" means "god of ugly things" in the local Maori language.

8. Females lay eggs in the soil of the forest floor.

9. Like other insects, giant wetas don't have lungs.

10. Instead, they breathe through their exoskeletons.

11. A weta's ears are located behind the knees on its front legs.

12. Wetas have been living on earth since before some dinosaurs lived.

GIANT WATER BUG

1. Giant water bugs live in ponds, slow-moving streams, and marshes all over the world.

2. They usually hide under clumps of plant matter.

3. The largest species of water bug can be more than 4.5 inches (12 cm) long.

4. These insects eat small fish, tadpoles, and insects.

5. They can kill and eat prey much bigger than themselves.

6. A giant water bug grabs prey with its long front legs.

7. Then it injects venomous saliva into its victim and sucks out the liquefied matter inside.

8. The bug's back legs are flat and covered with tiny hairs called cilia.

9. The back legs' shape and the cilia help the giant water bug swim.

10. A giant water bug has a long tube that sticks out of the water so it can breathe underwater.

11. Water bugs also hold air bubbles under their wings to breathe underwater.

12. Females lay more than 100 eggs at a time.

13. Unlike many other insects, the male takes care of the eggs.

14. In one species, the male carries the eggs on its back.

15. In another, the male watches over eggs laid on leaves.

16. Giant water bugs sometimes bite people between their toes.

17. They can defend themselves by playing dead or squirting a nasty-smelling liquid from their butts.

GIANT ANTEATER

1. This odd-looking creature really is a giant.

2. It can measure up to 8 feet (2.4 meters) long and is the largest of the four anteater species.

3. Anteaters have no teeth.

4. Instead, they suck up ants with their super-long tongue.

5. Anteaters tear a hole in anthill with sharp, 4-inch-long (10 cm) claws, then they stick their head in and start slurping.

6. An anteater can flick its tongue up to 150 times a minute.

7. It has to eat quickly, because the ants fight back with painful stings.

8. Giant anteaters have one baby each year.

9. The baby sometimes rides on its mother's back.

10. Giant anteaters are shy, but they will fight if they have to.

11. When it fights, an anteater will stand up on its back legs and use its sharp claws.

12. A cornered anteater can even fight off a jaguar.

GECKO

1. Geckos live on every continent except Antarctica.

2. They live in rain forests, mountains, and deserts.

3. There are more than 1,500 different species of geckos.

4. A gecko's long tail helps it balance as it runs.

5. This lizard also stores fat in its tail.

6. If a predator grabs the gecko's tail, the tail will fall off.

7. The tail wiggles and moves around for a while, giving the gecko the chance to escape.

8. Geckos have sticky hairs on their toes.

9. These hairs let them climb up walls and even walk upside-down.

10. Geckos munch on insects.

11. Some also eat fruit and nectar.

12. A gecko has no eyelids. Instead, a thin membrane covers its eyes.

13. The gecko keeps the membrane clean by licking it with its tongue.

14. Geckos make chirping or clicking noises.

15. They also bob their heads to communicate with each other.

1. This reptile is also called the gharial.

2. It has a long, narrow snout.

3. Rows of sharp teeth stick out even when the animal's mouth is closed.

4. The gavial sweeps its long snout through the water to catch fish.

5. Special sensors in their scales help them detect a fish's motion.

6. Gavials are the longest members of the crocodile family.

7. They can be between 13 and 21 feet (4 to 6.5 meters) long.

8. Males have an organ called the ghara on their throat.

9. The ghara makes sounds louder, which helps the male attract a mate.

10. Gavials lay the largest eggs in the crocodile family.

11. An egg weighs about 6 ounces (67 grams).

12. Females lay between 30 and 60 eggs at a time.

13. The gavial's webbed feet help it swim.

14. Even though it spends most of its time in the water, a gavial also likes to sunbathe on logs.

15. These animals once lived all over Southeast Asia, but today they only live in parts of Nepal, India, and Bangladesh.

GAVIAL

FULMAR

1. This bird's beak has something extra!

2. The fulmar has a "nostril" on top of its beak.

3. Inside is a special gland that lets the bird remove salt from its body.

4. Fulmars need this gland because they swallow a lot of salty ocean water when they dive.

5. "Fulmar" comes from an old Norse word meaning "foul gull."

6. But the fulmar isn't a gull at all. It's more closely related to a bird called the albatross.

7. The fulmar can be foul, though. It spits a nasty-smelling oil to keep other animals from getting too close.

8. Fulmars live off the coast of several European nations.

9. These seabirds glide over the sea on stiff wings, looking for fish to eat.

10. Fulmars build nests on high cliffs.

11. They fly straight up to reach these high nests.

12. Fulmars are one of the few birds with a great sense of smell.

13. This sense helps them find food.

14. Fulmars can live for more than 30 years.

15. Large flocks of these birds often follow fishing boats to grab some food.

FRILLED LIZARD

1. This lizard has a fancy way to scare away predators.

2. It uncurls a large flap, or frill, around its neck.

3. The lizard also stands on its hind legs and opens its mouth wide.

4. If these efforts to look big and scary don't work, the lizard will turn around and run away on two legs.

5. The frill also helps the lizard control its body temperature.

6. Frilled lizards only live in Australia.

7. They spend most of their time in trees but come down to the ground to hunt.

8. Frilled lizards eat insects, spiders, and small lizards and mammals.

9. These reptiles can be up to 3 feet (1 meter) long.

10. They only weigh about a pound (0.45 kg).

11. Females lay between 8 and 23 eggs in an underground nest.

12. The temperature of the nest determines what sex the babies will be.

13. Warm temperatures produce more females.

14. The babies can take care of themselves—and even display that big frill—as soon as they hatch.

FOUR-EYED FISH

1. Despite its name, this fish does not wear glasses.

2. Instead, it has special eyes.

3. This fish's eyes are on top of its head.

4. They are divided into two parts by a thin strip of tissue.

5. The top part of the eyes can see on land, while the bottom part can see underwater.

6. Four-eyed fish live near the surface of rivers and coastal waters in Central and South America.

7. This fish hunts underwater for algae, insects, crabs, and worms.

8. When it sees prey in the air, it will jump out of the water to grab it.

9. Four-eyed fish will even drag themselves onto land to feed.

10. These fish are active during the day.

11. They gather in large groups of 100 or more.

12. Instead of laying eggs, like most fish do, four-eyed fish give birth to live young.

FLYING SQUIRREL

1. The flying squirrel doesn't really fly.

2. But it can glide from tree to tree just like a bird.

3. The secret is a flap of furry skin that stretches between each wrist and ankle.

4. A flying squirrel can glide up to 300 feet (91 meters) and turn in the air.

5. Flying squirrels live in forests and woods all over North America.

6. Some species live in Asia.

7. Holes in trees or empty nests make great homes for these little creatures.

8. In winter, sometimes several flying squirrels will nest together to keep warm. Cuddles!

9. Flying squirrels often fall prey to owls, hawks, or tree-climbing mammals.

10. These squirrels are omnivores, which means they eat just about anything.

11. Favorite foods are insects, seeds, nuts, fruit, eggs, birds, and even dead animals.

12. Flying squirrels are common, but because they are nocturnal, most people never see them.

13. Their big eyes help them see in the dark.

14. Flying squirrels glow under ultraviolet light. Scientists aren't sure why.

FLYING FOX

1. These creatures aren't foxes at all. They are bats.

2. Flying foxes get their name because their heads look a lot like fox heads.

3. Flying foxes are also called fruit bats.

4. They eat—You guessed it!—fruit.

5. Flying foxes are active at night.

6. They spread seeds from the fruit they eat.

7. The seeds pass through their digestive system and fall to the ground in their poop.

8. Flying foxes are the largest members of the bat family. They are part of a group called megabats.

9. These bats can be up to 16 inches (40 cm) long.

10. Their wingspan can be up to 5 feet (1.5 meters).

11. A group of flying foxes is called a camp.

12. A camp can include thousands of bats.

13. To cool down on a hot day, a flying fox will skim over a river or lake, then lick the water from its belly.

14. Flying foxes are good swimmers.

15. These bats can't take off from the ground.

16. Instead, they have to climb a tree to get enough height to fly.

17. Flying foxes live in hot places in Southeast Asia and Australia.

18. They can fly as fast as 19 miles (31 km) an hour.

19. A bat's wing is nothing like a bird's wing.

20. It is made of skin stretched between thin bones.

21. A flying fox's thumb has a long claw, which it uses for grooming and climbing.

22. It wraps its wings around itself to keep warm while it sleeps.

23. Unlike other bats, flying foxes don't use echolocation because they don't hunt moving insects.

24. Instead, their excellent sense of smell helps them find food.

1. Fleas have been around for millions of years.

2. There is evidence of flea bites on dinosaur fossils from 165 million years ago.

3. Fleas are real vampires—sucking blood is their main activity.

4. One flea can feed up to 15 times a day.

5. Fleas can't fly. But they sure can jump!

6. A flea can jump about 150 times its height.

7. Fleas are great jumpers because they store energy in their legs, then release it all at once.

8. Fleas only live about 100 days.

9. During that time, a female flea can lay up to 500 eggs.

10. Hundreds of years ago, people enjoyed watching flea circuses.

11. They watched fleas jump and pull tiny carts.

12. Flea bites aren't just itchy.

13. The bites are dangerous too, because fleas spread many diseases.

FLEA

FLATWORM

1. A flatworm isn't actually flat.
2. Its body is round, with a flat underside.
3. Flatworms live in small pools.
4. They feed on tiny worms, protozoa, and bacteria.
5. A flatworm's mouth is on the underside of its body.
6. It sticks its mouth into its prey and sucks out its insides.
7. Then the food travels straight to the flatworm's stomach.
8. The flatworm pushes waste out of its body through the same opening.
9. A flatworm is covered with tiny hairs called cilia.
10. The cilia act like tiny oars and let the flatworm move along the surface of the water.

FLAMINGO

1. A flamingo has the second-longest legs of any bird.

2. Those legs can be 31 to 49 inches (80 to 125 cm) long.

3. That's longer than the bird's body!

4. A flamingo can stand up to 59 inches (150 cm) tall.

5. A flamingo's ankle is halfway up its leg.

6. And its knee is next to its body.

7. Flamingos are often seen resting on one leg, and scientists still aren't sure why.

8. Most flamingos have three toes that face forward and one toe that faces backward.

9. That hind toe is called a hallux.

10. Flamingos have webbed feet.

11. The webbing helps stir up food in the water.

12. Flamingos get their pink color from the beta-carotene in the food they eat.

13. Their favorite foods are algae, shrimp, protozoa, worms, and plants.

14. Flamingos in zoos lose their pink color unless they are given beta-carotene.

15. There are 19 vertebrae in a flamingo's long neck.

16. A flamingo's bill filters food out of the water by holding its bill upside-down so water drains out.

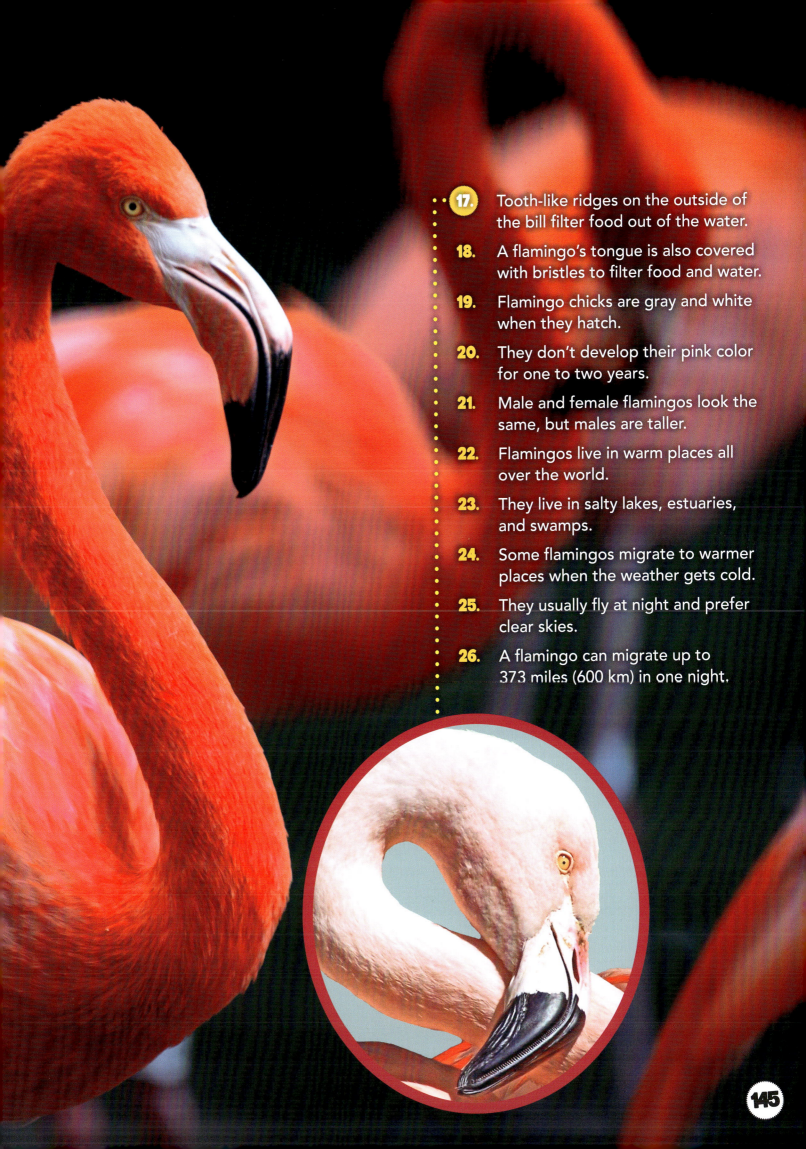

17. Tooth-like ridges on the outside of the bill filter food out of the water.

18. A flamingo's tongue is also covered with bristles to filter food and water.

19. Flamingo chicks are gray and white when they hatch.

20. They don't develop their pink color for one to two years.

21. Male and female flamingos look the same, but males are taller.

22. Flamingos live in warm places all over the world.

23. They live in salty lakes, estuaries, and swamps.

24. Some flamingos migrate to warmer places when the weather gets cold.

25. They usually fly at night and prefer clear skies.

26. A flamingo can migrate up to 373 miles (600 km) in one night.

FIRE-BELLIED TOAD

1. Fire-bellied toads are green and black on top, but the undersides of their bodies have a surprise!

2. Their undersides are bright red, orange, and black.

3. These toads flip onto their backs to show off those colors when a predator attacks.

4. The bright colors warn predators that the toad is poisonous.

5. Its skin gives off a milky liquid that irritates the attacker's mouth and eyes.

6. Fire-bellied toads live in China, Russia, and Korea.

7. They are only about 2 inches (6 cm) long.

8. These amphibians spend most of their time in slow-moving streams and ponds.

9. They hibernate in rotting logs or piles of dead leaves during the winter.

10. Unlike most toads, this creature cannot stretch out its tongue to catch insects.

11. Instead, the toad catches its prey by grabbing it in its mouth.

12. When looking for a mate, males float on top of the water with their legs stretched out and make a "ting-ting" sound to attract females.

13. Fire-bellied toads live longer than most other toad species.

14. They can live for 12 to 15 years in the wild, and even longer in captivity.

EMU

1. This tall bird lives in Australia.
2. It can be up to 6.6 feet (2 meters) tall.
3. Emus have wings, but they cannot fly.
4. The emu is great at running, though.
5. It can run as fast as 31 miles (50 km) an hour.
6. It is also able to run over long distances.
7. Emus are the second-largest bird in the world. Only the ostrich is larger.
8. Emus may not use their wings to fly, but they are useful for other things.
9. Emus stretch out their wings to stay cool.
10. The wings also help the emu balance as it runs.
11. An emu has two sets of eyelids.
12. One set blinks, and the other keeps out dust and dirt.
13. Emus like to eat plants and insects like grasshoppers, cockroaches, and beetles.
14. They don't stay in one place for long. Instead, they move on to find more food.
15. Emus used to be hunted for their meat. Today, emu meat comes from birds raised on farms.

ELEPHANT SEAL

1. There are two species of elephant seal.

2. The southern elephant seal is the largest seal in the world.

3. A male can weigh more than 8,800 pounds (3,992 kg) and be almost 20 feet (9 meters) long.

4. Males are much larger than females.

5. These seals live in the freezing waters of the Antarctic.

6. The water may be cold, but it is full of the fish and squid the seals like to eat.

7. The seals only come onshore to breed.

8. The northern elephant seal is the second largest species.

9. They live off the coast of California.

10. The elephant seal gets its name from the male's nose, which looks kind of like an elephant's trunk.

11. A male elephant seal hangs out with 40 to 50 females in a group called a colony.

12. Males often fight each other to defend their territory.

13. Females give birth to a single pup in the winter after a pregnancy that lasts 11 months.

14. These animals keep warm using a thick layer of fat, called blubber, under their skin.

15. They can hold their breath for up to 100 minutes.

16. Seals lose patches of hair and skin through a process called molting.

17. During molting, the seals can't go in the cold water. Instead, they find a safe place on land until their skin grows back.

148

ELECTRIC EEL

1. Surprise! Electric eels aren't eels at all. They are fish.

2. Electric eels have very poor eyesight. But that doesn't stop them from finding prey.

3. Instead of looking for food, these eels give off a weak electric signal to find their way around.

4. They also use this signal to find a mate.

5. When an electric eel finds prey, it stuns it with a powerful electric charge.

6. That shock can measure up to 650 volts—more than five times stronger than the current that powers your home.

7. These creatures have three organs that produce electricity.

8. These organs take up 80 percent of its body.

9. Electric eels grow to be about 8 feet (2.4 meters) long.

10. They live in the muddy waters of the Amazon River and other parts of South America.

11. A group of electric eels is called a swarm.

ECHIDNA

1. Like many other oddball animals, echidnas are only found in Australia.

2. It is part of an animal group called monotremes.

3. Monotremes are mammals that lay eggs. Weird!

4. These creatures are named after a creature from Greek mythology named Echidna, who was called the "Mother of Monsters."

5. That seems harsh, since echidnas are actually really cute.

6. Their little bodies are covered with short prickly spikes.

7. These spikes are made of tough hair.

8. There are two types of echidna: long-beaked and short-beaked.

9. You can tell them apart by their nose.

10. An echidna has no teeth.

11. It uses its sharp claws to tear up anthills and termite mounds, then slurps up the insects with its long, sticky tongue.

12. An echidna's tongue can be 6 inches (15 cm) long.

13. An echidna has rough pads on the roof of its mouth to help it break down food.

14. They also eat insect larvae and worms.

15. An echidna can scarf down 40,000 insects a day.

16. These creatures have the second-lowest body temperature in the world.

17. Only the platypus's body temperature is lower.

18. They also have a very slow metabolism and don't move very fast.

19. Echidnas can live up to 45 years in the wild.

20. They waddle when they walk.

21. A female echidna lays one egg into a pouch on her body.

22. The egg hatches after about 10 days.

23. A baby echidna is called a puggle.

24. At first, a puggle is about the size of a jellybean.

25. It spends about seven weeks in its mother's pouch.

26. When the puggle gets bigger and starts to get spiky, Mom leaves it in an underground burrow.

27. When it is frightened, an echidna will curl up into a ball.

EARWIG

1. There are about 2,000 species of earwig.

2. They are found all over the world.

3. Ten species live in the United States.

4. This insect's sharp pincers make it look scary, but it is actually harmless.

5. Although earwigs can damage plants, they also eat harmful insects called aphids.

6. Female earwigs are good moms, which is very unusual in the insect world.

7. A female guards its eggs for several weeks.

8. She will even groom the eggs to remove harmful fungi.

9. Once the eggs hatch, the baby nymphs stay with their mother until they are bigger.

10. One species of earwig, called the hump earwig, takes mothering to the extreme.

11. This species' larvae eat their own mother. Yikes!

12. Male earwigs have curved pincers, but a female's pincers are straight.

13. Earwigs may get their name from an old superstition that says they will crawl into a person's ear and use their pincers to burrow into the brain. Fortunately, this is not true!

1. Earthworms spend most of their lives underground.

2. They dig tunnels under the soil.

3. These tunnels help bring air into the soil, which makes the soil healthier.

4. Their slimy bodies also put nitrogen into the soil, which is an important nutrient for plants.

5. When it rains, the tunnels flood, and the earthworms come out, which is why you see so many after a storm.

6. An earthworm's body is divided into segments called annuli.

7. Hairy bristles help them move through the soil.

8. Earthworms eat soil.

9. They can eat up to a third of their body weight in one day.

10. Inside its body, a long tube runs from its mouth to its butt.

11. You can find more than a million earthworms in 1 acre (0.4 hectare) of land.

12. Baby worms hatch from tiny cocoons that are smaller than a grain of rice.

13. If part of an earthworm's body is cut off, it often grows back.

14. Worms don't have eyes, but they can sense light.

15. They have no lungs and no bones.

EARTHWORM

ODDBALL

FAST FACTS!

10 WEIRD EXTINCT ANIMALS

1. **Argentavis:** The largest flying bird that ever lived, Argentavis had a 24-foot (7-meter) wingspan.

2. **Glyptodon:** Imagine an armadillo the size of a Volkswagen Beetle! Glyptodons were huge, armored mammals covered with thick armor and spikes. Oh, and they had a clubbed tail too.

3. **Megalania:** Can you picture a 23-foot (7-meter) lizard that weighed more than 4,000 pounds (1,814 kg)? Say hello to Megalania, a giant that roamed Australia millions of years ago.

4. **Ground Sloth:** Today's sloths have got nothing on their ancient ancestor! Ground sloths were about 20 feet (6 meters) long and weighed around 9,000 pounds (4,082 kg). They roamed Earth as recently as 10,000 years ago and were probably hunted by prehistoric humans.

5. **Daeodon:** These prehistoric pigs belong to a group called "terminator pigs." At 6 feet (1.8 meters) tall and weighing thousands of pounds (kg), these aren't animals anyone would want to mess with.

6. **Giant Otter:** When scientists in China found an entire skull of this ancient creature, they figured out it was probably the size of a wolf. That's a lot bigger than the cute otters we have around today.

7. **Giant Beaver:** These big boys were the size of a black bear. They roamed North America until about 11,000 years ago, no doubt cutting down giant trees.

8. **Megalodon:** This big-mouthed shark was 50 feet (15 meters) long and had 7-inch (18-cm) teeth. Two adult humans could fit inside its giant mouth. Megalodon was at the top of the food chain and even preyed on whales.

9. **Terror Birds:** The name pretty much says it all. Scientists think this ancient bird was 10 feet (3 meters) tall and could kill prey just by cracking their skulls with one blow from its powerful beak.

10. **Meganeura:** These giant dragonflies probably looked a lot like today's insects—but super-sized! Meganeura's wingspan was a whopping 2 feet (0.6 meter) wide.

DUNG BEETLE

1. The dung beetle has a strange relationship with other animals' poop, or dung.

2. They eat it, live in it, and lay their eggs in it.

3. There are three kinds of dung beetles: rollers, tunnelers, and dwellers. Each type has a different way of dealing with poop.

4. Rollers push poop into a ball and roll it away to snack on later.

5. Pairs of tunnelers dig a tunnel under the ball of poop.

6. The female stays underground, while the male sends down bits of poopy snacks.

7. Dwellers actually live inside the poop, so they have their favorite food 24-7.

8. Dung beetles lay their eggs inside the poop.

9. The larvae eat the poop after they hatch.

10. Poop is full of nutrients and undigested food.

11. A male dung beetle has horns on its head.

12. It uses the horns to fight other males.

13. Dung beetles are among the strongest animals on Earth.

14. They can move more than 1,000 times their own weight.

DIVING BELL SPIDER

1. This creature is the only spider that spends almost its whole life underwater.

2. It builds a web underwater, then carries air bubbles into the web to fill it with oxygen to breathe.

3. Tiny hairs on the spider's abdomen trap air bubbles.

4. Diving bell spiders live in Europe and Asia.

5. They only live in fresh water.

6. These spiders lay their eggs on plants in the water.

7. Males are much larger than females.

8. Females lay between 30 and 60 eggs in an egg sac underwater.

9. These spiders are carnivores.

10. They eat insect larvae, water mites, and tiny crustaceans.

DARWIN'S FROG

1. The Darwin's frog lives in forests and streams in Chile and Argentina.

2. It is named after scientist Charles Darwin, who discovered it during the 1830s.

3. These frogs look like dead leaves, which helps them hide from predators on the forest floor.

4. After a female lays her eggs, the male carries the tiny tadpoles in his vocal sac.

5. The tadpoles stay in the vocal sac for 50 to 70 days.

6. These frogs are tiny, growing only about 1.5 inches (4 cm) long.

7. They are speedy, hopping along at up to 5 miles (8 km) an hour.

8. Although its body is round, the Darwin's frog's head is shaped like a triangle.

9. Its back feet are webbed, which helps the frog swim.

10. The Darwin's frog is an ambush hunter.

11. It sits quietly until an insect, snail, worm, or spider gets too close.

12. Then—zap!—the frog snatches its prey with its sticky tongue.

13. A fungus may have killed off one species of Darwin's frog.

CUTTLEFISH

1. Cuttlefish are mollusks.

2. They are related to octopuses and squid.

3. Cuttlefish have three hearts.

4. Two hearts pump blood to the cuttlefish's gills, while the third pumps the oxygenated blood around the body.

5. Cuttlefish have excellent eyesight.

6. They can see behind them.

7. They can also see in very low light.

8. And they can see wavelengths of light humans can't.

9. They change the shape of their eyes as they look around.

10. Cuttlefish can change color.

11. They are sometimes called the "chameleons of the sea."

12. The weird thing is, cuttlefish are color-blind, yet they can change color to match their surroundings.

13. They can even change color in the dark.

14. Both male and female cuttlefish die shortly after they mate and the female lays eggs.

15. A large fin around the cuttlefish's body makes it a fast swimmer.

16. These creatures can also squirt water to move very quickly.

CUCKOO WASP

1. This tiny insect has an oddball way of caring for its babies.

2. It lays its eggs in the nest of another species of wasp.

3. The cuckoo wasp's larvae hatch first, then eat the host wasp's larvae's food.

4. Sometimes the cuckoo wasp larvae eat the other larvae too.

5. The cuckoo wasp is named after the cuckoo bird.

6. These insects are only about 0.5 inch (1.2 cm) long.

7. Cuckoo wasps are a bright metallic green or blue.

8. These wasps have a flexible abdomen.

9. They can curl up into a ball when threatened.

10. The wasp's body is covered with hard plates that work like armor.

11. Cuckoo wasps don't sting.

12. They sip nectar from flowers.

13. These wasps are found all over the world.

CUCKOO

1. There are more than 125 different species of cuckoo.

2. These birds live all over the world.

3. They get their name from the sound they make.

4. Some species of cuckoos don't raise their own babies.

5. They don't even bother to build nests.

6. Females lay 12 to 22 eggs in other birds' nests.

7. A female will usually lay her eggs in the same species of bird that raised her.

8. Sometimes the cuckoo chicks will push other chicks out of the nest, so they can have all of the mother's attention.

9. Cuckoos eat caterpillars, grasshoppers, and other insects.

10. They walk around the ground to find food.

CRUCIFIX TOAD

1. This toad is also called the Holy Cross toad.

2. It gets its name from the spots on its back, which are in the shape of a cross.

3. Crucifix toads live in Australia.

4. This tiny creature is only 2.5 inches (6.5 cm) long.

5. They live in underground burrows.

6. Its feet are shaped like shovels.

7. The Crucifix toad can dig up to 10 feet (3 meters) underground.

8. To stay wet, this toad builds a moist cocoon around itself.

9. It can remain dormant in this cocoon for months or even years.

10. When rain finally trickles underground, the toad eats its own cocoon.

11. Then large numbers of these creatures come above ground to feed and mate.

12. They don't have much time, as adults only live for six to eight weeks.

13. Crucifix toads eat mosquito larvae, insects, and tadpoles.

14. They wiggle their toes in the water to lure their prey close.

15. A Crucifix toad's skin gives off a sticky substance that traps flies.

16. As it gets bigger, it sheds its skin and eats it—insects and all.

17. This substance also tastes bad, which keeps predators away.

1. Crickets are very lightweight. They weigh less than a paper clip.

2. These insects have powerful back legs.

3. They can jump 30 times their length in one leap.

4. Crickets don't have lungs. Instead, they breathe through holes in their exoskeleton.

5. Every species of cricket has its own unique chirp.

6. Crickets chirp by rubbing their wings together.

7. Each wing has 50 to 300 rough bumps that make noise when rubbed together.

8. Only male crickets chirp. They chirp to attract mates.

9. A special organ called the tympanum picks up chirping sounds.

10. The tympanum is located on the cricket's front legs.

11. The tympanum also alerts the cricket if danger is approaching.

12. Crickets chirp faster in warm weather than in cold.

13. If you count a cricket's chirps in one minute, then divide that number by four and add 40, you will have the approximate temperature (in degrees Fahrenheit). Try it!

14. Crickets are sometimes kept as pets in China.

15. They are considered to be good luck.

16. Some people enjoy fighting crickets as a sport.

CRICKET

CONE SNAIL

1. Cone snails live in warm oceans all over the world.

2. They measure about 6 inches (15 cm) long.

3. Their pretty shells are popular with collectors.

4. There are about 500 different species.

5. They usually lie in the sand during the day and come out at night to find food.

6. They are carnivores and eat worms and fish.

7. Touching or stepping on a cone snail can be a painful experience.

8. These creatures have one long, sharp tooth that is attached to the body by a thin tissue.

9. When they sense prey, they shoot the tooth out like a harpoon to stab it.

10. The cone snail's venom paralyzes the prey, and the snail gobbles it up.

11. Two species, the geography cone and the textile cone, have venom powerful enough to kill a person.

12. There is no antidote to cone snail venom. The best a victim can do is stay alive until the poison wears off.

CICADA

1. These insects spend most of their lives underground.

2. Adult cicadas deposit their eggs on tree branches.

3. The young, called nymphs, hatch and then fall to the ground.

4. They stay underground for many years, sucking on water from tree roots to stay alive.

5. Finally, as the soil warms up in late spring, the cicadas emerge.

6. Cicadas emerge in huge groups called broods.

7. There can be billions of cicadas in a brood.

8. The insects climb trees and make a loud noise to attract a mate.

9. Their buzzing can be louder than a lawn mower or a chainsaw.

10. About six weeks later, after the females lay their eggs, they all die.

11. Cicadas stay underground for 13 to 17 years.

12. Some cultures think cicadas make a tasty and crunchy food.

CHEVROTAIN

1. This creature is sometimes called the mouse deer, and it's easy to see why.

2. A chevrotain weighs about 10 pounds (4.5 kg) and is the size of a rabbit.

3. They stand only 12 inches (30 cm) tall.

4. Chevrotains aren't deer at all. They are their own unique animal family.

5. Chevrotains are the smallest hoofed mammal in the world.

6. They live in forests in Southeast Asia and Africa.

7. Chevrotains don't have horns or antlers. But they do have fangs!

8. The males of some species have curved tusks that they use for fighting.

9. Some chevrotains are good swimmers.

10. They can walk around underwater for several minutes to avoid predators.

11. These little dudes can jump straight up in the air when frightened.

12. They eat insects, leaves, and fruit.

13. Chevrotains are mostly active at night.

14. They first appeared on Earth 34 million years ago.

CHAMELEON

1. There are more than 200 species of chameleon.

2. Most live on the island of Madagascar.

3. They range in size from 2 feet (0.6 meter) to just 1.1 inch (30 mm) long.

4. Chameleons have super-weird eyes.

5. Each eye can move separately in different directions, so the lizard can look at two things at once.

6. A chameleon's sticky tongue is about twice as long as its body.

7. It keeps its tongue curled up in the back of its mouth.

8. When an insect comes close, the chameleon's tongue zips out to catch it.

9. A chameleon's skin has crystal-like cells that absorb all colors of light.

10. These cells allow the chameleon to change color.

11. Males become brighter to attract females or to scare away other males.

12. Changing color may also help these cold-blooded reptiles to regulate their body temperature.

13. Chameleons use their five-toed feet and strong tails to climb and hang from tree branches.

ODDBALL FAST FACTS!

25 UNUSUAL WAYS ANIMALS COMMUNICATE

1. Bees wiggle in a butt-shaking dance to tell other bees where to find food.

2. Many male birds perform elaborate dances to tell female birds they are interested in them.

3. Fireflies flash their lights to attract mates.

4. Male peacock spiders perform a high-kicking dance to impress their female counterparts.

5. Squids and octopuses change color to send messages to other creatures.

6. Squids can even display one color on one side of their bodies and another color on the other side. Talk about sending mixed messages!

7. Mantis shrimp have color receptors that only other mantis shrimp can see. They move their arms and legs to make different-colored light bounce off them to send messages.

8. African elephants make sounds that are too low for humans to hear.

9. A tarsier can make sounds that are way too high for human ears to hear.

10. The African demon mole rat lives underground and sends messages to other mole rats by banging its head on the roof of its tunnel. Headbangers, unite!

11. Some fish, like the Peters's elephantnose fish and the black ghost knifefish, have electroreceptors that can pick up electrical signals from other fish.

12. White rhinos poop in big piles. When other rhinos stop by, they take a good, long sniff to see what other rhinos have been there.

13. Dogs also communicate by smelling each other and objects dogs have marked with their urine.

14. Insects called treehoppers produce a sweet liquid called honeydew. Day geckos think honeydew is a sweet treat! When a day gecko wants a snack, it will bob its head up and down until the treehopper shoots a tasty piece of honeydew right into the lizard's mouth.

15. Asian wild dogs called dholes communicate by whistling, shrieking, and making loud clicking noises.

16. Silverback gorillas hum to call their families to dinner. Try this next time it's time to eat!

17. Whales and dolphins communicate by clicking. Creatures who live in different parts of the ocean have different accents.

18. Chimpanzees groom each other to show affection. There's nothing like picking insects off a friend to show you care.

19. An ape called the bonobo uses body language—waving arms, pointing, and shaking their heads—to get their point across.

20. Ants use special chemicals called pheromones to communicate with each other by smell.

21. Seahorses vibrate and make tiny growling noises when they are upset.

22. Cats meow, of course, but only to communicate with people. They do not meow at other cats.

23. White-tailed deer flick up their tails to alert other deer to danger. When other deer see that white patch under the tail, they know it's time to be alert.

24. A dolphin will slap the water with its tail to get other dolphins' attention.

25. Elephants wrap their trunks around each other to show affection.

BURYING BEETLE

1. This beetle is great at cleaning up messes.

2. Males fly at night to find carcasses, or dead animals.

3. They give off a scent that attracts a female.

4. The male and female work together to bury the carcass.

5. Sometimes the beetles roll the carcass into a ball and carry it to a nest somewhere else.

6. They do this by lying on their backs and balancing the carcass above them while they walk.

7. A burying beetle can carry up to 200 times its own weight.

8. The male and female mate, and the female lays her eggs in or near the carcass.

9. Females stay with the eggs and larvae.

10. When the eggs hatch, the larvae have a tasty, but dead, animal to feed on.

1. We think of birds living in trees, but the burrowing owl has a different idea.

2. These birds burrow, or live in holes under the ground.

3. Sometimes they live in abandoned prairie dog burrows.

4. They can also use their strong front feet and claws to dig their own burrows.

5. Burrowing owls live in grasslands and deserts in the western United States, as well as in some parts of Central and South America.

6. They are one of the smallest owls, measuring just 9 inches (23 cm) tall.

7. They eat small mammals, lizards, birds, and insects.

8. They line their burrows with grass and dirt to make them cozy.

9. Burrowing owls also place animal poop in or near their burrows.

10. Then they eat the dung beetles that come to eat the poop.

11. These birds can make a noise like a rattlesnake to scare away predators.

12. They are one of the few owl species that is active during the day.

BURROWING OWL

BROWN PELICAN

1. This bird has a big mouth for real! A large pouch hangs from the bottom of its bill.

2. Pelicans fly above the water, looking for fish down below.

3. When a pelican spots a fish, it tucks in its wings and dives straight down like a torpedo.

4. Air sacs under the bird's skin cushion the landing.

5. A pelican stores fish and water in its pouch.

6. Its pouch can hold up to three gallons of fish and water.

7. When the pelican lands, it drains the water from its pouch.

8. Then it flips the fish around and swallows it headfirst.

9. A large hook at the tip of the pelican's beak helps hold wiggly fish still.

10. Pelicans, like other marine birds, need to remove salt from the seawater they drink.

11. To do this, pelicans have special glands on the side of their heads, above their eyes.

12. Salty water flows down grooves in the pelican's bill.

13. Pelicans have great eyesight. They can spot fish from 65 feet (20 meters) up in the air.

14. Brown pelicans are one of two pelican species that dive to catch fish.

15. The other diving species is the Peruvian pelican.

16. All other pelican species sit on the water and snatch up fish that swim past.

17. Brown pelicans live near coastal waters around North and South America.

18. Their wings stretch about 7 feet (over 2 meters) wide.

19. Sometimes pelicans fly in lines just above the water.

20. This arrangement compresses the air so each pelican doesn't have to work hard to fly.

21. Male pelicans look for a mate during the fall.

22. When they are looking, their pouch turns bright red to attract a female.

23. A pesticide called DDT endangered the brown pelican because it made their eggshells too thin for the baby birds to survive.

24. A law banned DDT in the United States in 1972. Since then, brown pelicans have made a big comeback.

3

BOWERBIRD

1. Male bowerbirds work very hard to get a mate.

2. Males build fancy nests called bowers out of sticks.

3. But that's not fancy enough to attract a female.

4. The males decorate the bowers to make them look nicer.

5. They add flowers, feathers, colored stones, and even wings from insects.

6. They use bottle caps and pen caps too.

7. Bowerbirds prefer blue objects.

8. Some even mix their saliva with plant material to make "paint" to add color.

9. Females inspect different nests, then pick the nest—and the male—they like best.

10. Once a female enters a bower, the male dances in front of it holding a colorful object in his mouth.

11. Bowerbirds live in Australia and New Guinea.

12. They mostly eat fruit but sometimes snack on insects, grubs, and seeds.

13. These birds are real chatterboxes. They make many different sounds.

14. Bowerbirds can even mimic human noises.

1. This little insect packs a mighty … squirt.

2. When it is threatened, the beetle releases a nasty chemical from its rear end.

3. The chemical irritates the eyes of predators. It also makes it hard for them to breathe.

4. The beetle's chemical is strong enough to burn human skin.

5. A bombardier is someone who releases bombs from an airplane. It's easy to see how this beetle got its name.

6. Scientists have seen frogs throw up these beetles when they realized how awful they taste.

7. Most of the beetles survive this nasty experience.

8. Bombardier beetles store their nasty chemicals in their abdomen. A valve releases the chemicals when the beetle is attacked.

9. The beetle can release up to 500 chemical bursts a second.

10. Bombardier beetles live in North America, South America, Europe, Australia, and Africa.

BOMBARDIER BEETLE

BOLAS SPIDER

1. A bola is a weapon made of a rope and weights.

2. The Bolas spider uses its thread like a bola to catch its prey.

3. The Bolas spider spins a sticky thread. The thread smells like a female moth.

4. The spider twirls the thread around when it senses movement.

5. If a male moth comes close, the spider hits it with its sticky thread.

6. Then it pulls the moth close and bites it.

7. The Bolas spider's bite paralyzes and kills the moth.

8. The spider might eat the moth right away. Or it might save it for later.

9. Bolas spiders are very tiny.

10. Females are larger than males.

11. These spiders live in Australia, Asia, Africa, and North and South America.

12. They are active at night and can see really well in the dark.

13. A female lays hundreds of eggs during her lifetime.

1. It's easy to see how this animal got its name. About half of its body is made up of a bright blue tail.

2. That blue color fades as the skink gets older.

3. Blue-tailed skinks are also called Western skinks.

4. They live in the western part of the United States and Canada.

5. A blue-tailed skink is only about 5 inches (13 cm) long.

6. Blue-tailed skinks are active during the day.

7. These lizards hunt insects, spiders, and earthworms.

8. If a predator grabs this skink by the tail, it's in for a big surprise! Skinks can shed their tails to escape from predators.

9. Later, the skink will grow a new tail.

10. Blue-tailed skinks like to bask in the sun on cold days.

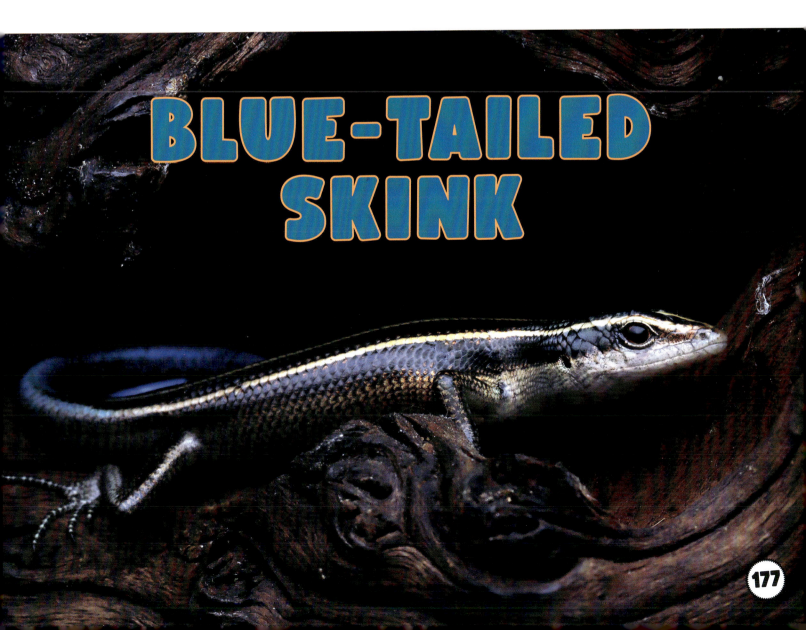

BLUE-TAILED SKINK

BLUE MORPHO BUTTERFLY

1. This pretty butterfly lives in the Amazon rainforest.

2. They also live in rainforests in Central America.

3. Only males are blue.

4. Females are brown, yellow, and black.

5. The bright blue color helps males defend their territory.

6. It also helps them attract females.

7. Surprise! Blue morphos aren't really blue. Their wings look blue because of the angle you are seeing them from.

8. Blue morphos are one of the largest butterfly species.

9. They measure 6 inches (15 cm) long.

10. A blue morpho's wingspan is up to 8 inches (20 cm) wide.

11. Only the top of the male butterfly's wings is blue.

12. Its underside is brown. This helps it hide from predators.

13. If it is threatened, the blue morpho lets loose with a smelly odor from glands on its front legs.

14. Blue morphos have smell receptors on their antenna.

15. They have taste receptors on their feet.

16. When they are caterpillars, blue morphos have teeth and chew on plants.

17. Adult blue morphos have no teeth.

18. Instead, they drink juice from rotting fruit, tree sap, even wet mud through a hollow tube called the proboscis.

19. Blue morphos only live about two weeks before laying eggs and dying.

20. Large swarms of these butterflies are so bright, they can actually be seen by pilots flying in planes over the rainforest.

21. Blue morphos are very active during the day.

22. At night, they find a cave or a hole in a tree, fold up their pretty wings, and go to sleep.

23. Scientists have studied blue morphos' light-reflecting ability to create new technology.

24. Some of this technology includes iridescent strips on money to discourage counterfeiting.

7

BLOBFISH

1. Blobfish have been called the world's ugliest animal.

2. They were first discovered in 2003 by a research vessel.

3. That first blobfish was named Mr. Blobby.

4. It is on display in the Australian Museum.

5. Blobfish are part of a family of fish called "fatheads."

6. Blobfish live in the deepest, darkest part of the ocean.

7. The water pressure deep in the ocean is 120 times what it is on land.

8. That strong pressure would squash a normal animal body. That's why blobfish look so weird.

9. A blobfish's body is mostly made of fat.

10. They do not have bones or muscles.

11. Blobfish look like normal fish when they are in the deep ocean.

12. When a blobfish is brought out of the ocean, its body collapses. That's why they look so droopy and, well, blobby.

13. Blobfish have no teeth.

14. They have big heads.

12 ....

15. They are only 12 inches (30 cm) long.

16. They weigh about 20 pounds (9 kg).

17. Blobfish are pretty lazy. They don't use their energy swimming or hunting.

18. Instead of swimming, blobfish just bob along on the water.

19. They eat small crabs and sea snails that float past.

20. Blobfish live in the waters around Australia and New Zealand.

21. Females lay thousands of soft, pink eggs on the ocean floor.

22. Both males and females lay on top of the eggs to protect them from predators.

23. Being lazy and living in a place with few predators mean the blobfish can live a very long time.

24. Scientists think these fish can live up to 130 years.

BLACK WIDOW SPIDER

1. There are three kinds of black widow spiders.

2. All of them live in the United States.

3. Not all black widows are black. Some are red or brown.

4. This spider is easy to identify because it has a red hourglass shape on its body.

5. Black widows are venomous.

6. A black widow spider's venom is 15 times more toxic than a rattlesnake's.

7. One bite from a black widow can kill a small animal.

8. People rarely die from a black widow bite, but they can get very sick from it.

9. Female black widows are larger and deadlier than males.

10. Baby black widow spiders are white. Their bodies get darker as they get older.

BLACK DRAGONFISH

1. Hundreds of years ago, sailors got glimpses of a creature they thought was a sea monster or a dragon. They thought the monster was huge and terrifying.

2. In 1877, scientists caught a real-life dragon in the North Atlantic Ocean. This creature became known as the black dragonfish.

3. The black dragonfish wasn't exactly huge. These fish are only about 20 inches (51 cm) long.

4. However, the fish has terrifying jaws and huge teeth. Pretty scary!

5. Only female black dragonfish have teeth.

6. A female's bite is stronger than a shark's.

7. Females come to the surface of the ocean to feed on other fish.

8. Males stay down in the depths of the ocean.

9. A male's skeleton is made of cartilage instead of bone.

10. Black dragonfish are luminescent. Parts of their bodies glow with light.

BINTURONG

1. Binturongs are also called bearcats.

2. But they aren't related to either bears or cats.

3. Bearcats live in Asia.

4. They eat almost anything, from berries to small animals.

5. They are great at climbing trees.

6. Binturongs have a leathery patch on the tip of their tails to help them climb.

7. They have what are called prehensile tails. That means they can be used for hanging or grabbing things.

8. Binturongs are about 3 feet (1 meter) long.

9. A binturong's tail is half the length of its body.

10. These animals spend most of their time up in trees.

11. Their tails help them hang on to branches while they sleep.

12. Binturongs smell like popcorn. But the reason is pretty disgusting.

13. That popcorn smell comes from a chemical in the animal's urine. That same chemical is found in popcorn.

14. Baby binturongs are called binlets.

15. Females give birth to one or two binlets at a time.

16. Binlets hang on to their mother's fur for the first few days of their lives.

BETTA

1. Bettas are also called Siamese fighting fish.

2. Their name comes from an ancient tribe of warriors called Bettah.

3. These fish are very territorial and will fight other fish that come too close.

4. Fish fighting was a popular sport in Thailand in the 1800s. Guess which fish were the champions of this odd sport?

5. Bettas live in rice paddies and slow-moving streams.

6. They have a special organ called the labyrinth that allows them to breathe air both above the surface and in the water.

7. Male betta fish make a small bubble on the surface of the water. They place their eggs there and guard the bubble until the eggs hatch.

8. These fish are great jumpers.

9. Many people keep betta fish as pets.

10. Each betta must be kept in a separate tank so they don't fight—and even kill—each other.

11. Bettas are very smart and can even learn tricks.

12. Wild bettas are dull-colored, but people have bred bettas in many different, bright colors.

BASILISK LIZARD

1. These lizards live near water in tropical rainforests.

2. They live in Central and South America.

3. Basilisks spend part of their time in trees and part of it in water.

4. Basilisks have long, flat toes on their back feet.

5. When they are frightened, these lizards stand up on their back legs and run.

6. They are quite speedy and can run as fast as 7 miles (11 km) per hour.

7. Basilisks have special scales on their feet.

8. These scales allow them to run on water.

9. Basilisks can hold their breath underwater for up to 10 minutes.

10. They can grow up to 3 feet (1 meter) long.

11. Their favorite foods are insects, spiders, smaller lizards, small mammals, and snails.

BABIRUSA

1. These wild pigs only live on a few Indonesian islands.

2. They live in tropical rainforests and swamps.

3. Their name comes from a Malay word for "hog deer."

4. Female pigs, called sows, do not have tusks.

5. Males have very large, long tusks on top of their nose and smaller tusks on their jaw.

6. The tusks look scary, but they are actually very brittle and break easily.

7. If a male's tusks don't break, they will grow so large they will pierce the animal's skull.

8. Males don't use their tusks to fight. Instead, they push each other around with their shoulders.

9. Sometimes they stand up and box each other with their front feet.

10. Males sharpen the tusks near their mouth by rubbing them on trees.

11. Babirusas are great swimmers.

12. They are also fast runners.

13. They use their strong front hooves to dig insects out of rotting trees and pull roots from the ground.

14. Babirusas like to wallow in mud to keep cool and get rid of insects that bite them.

AXOLOTL

1. These little cuties are a type of salamander.

2. Most salamanders lose their gills and breathe air when they grow up. But the axolotl keeps its gills for life.

3. That means axolotls can only survive in water.

4. Axolotls do have tiny lungs, but they don't use them.

5. These little creatures only live in freshwater lakes and canals near Mexico City.

6. The shape of an axolotl's mouth makes it look like it is always smiling.

7. Axolotls have no teeth.

8. They eat their prey by sucking it into their mouths.

9. Axolotls eat lots of different things, including worms, insects, small fish, and tiny crabs.

10. Baby axolotls sometimes eat their brothers and sisters after birth.

11. An axolotl can regrow body parts.

12. They can even regrow internal organs!

13. Females lay up to 1,000 eggs at a time.

14. The eggs float down to the bottom of the lake and stay there until they hatch.

15. Babies can take care of themselves right away.

16. Axolotls can change color to hide from predators.

1. These crabs are all legs! Arrow crabs have ten legs.

2. An arrow crab's body is only about 2 inches (5 cm) long. But its legs can be up to three times that size.

3. An arrow crab uses eight of its legs to walk around.

4. It uses its two front legs to eat and defend itself.

5. If a predator approaches, the arrow crab sticks its two front legs into a point to chase it away.

6. Arrow crabs live near sea urchins and anemones. They are safe from most predators there.

7. Arrow crabs eat worms and other tiny sea animals.

8. They also scavenge leftovers they find on the sea floor.

9. Don't mess with an arrow crab! These creatures are territorial and will chase intruders away.

10. Arrow crabs are invertebrates. They have a hard exoskeleton, or shell.

11. Baby arrow crabs do not have a shell. The hard covering develops later.

12. Arrow crabs live in coral reefs in the Caribbean and off the southeastern coasts of North and South America.

ARROW CRAB

ARMADILLO

1. Armadillo means "little armored one" in Spanish.

2. This animal got its name because it is covered in bony plates called a carapace.

3. Those plates are made of keratin. Human fingernails are also made of keratin.

4. There are about 20 species of armadillo.

5. The nine-banded armadillo is the only armadillo that lives in the United States.

6. Despite its name, these armadillos can also have three, seven, or eleven bands on their armor.

7. Nine-banded armadillos live in the southeastern part of the U.S.

8. Climate change means that these animals are moving farther north.

9. Nine-banded armadillos can hold their breath for up to six minutes.

10. This talent allows it to walk around underwater.

11. It can also swallow air to inflate its stomach and become more buoyant in water.

12. Nine-banded armadillos jump straight up in the air when they are surprised.

13. The three-banded armadillo, which lives in South America, can roll up into a ball.

14. If bony plates aren't protection enough, the screaming hairy armadillo makes a loud screeching noise when it is scared.

15. The smallest armadillo is the pink fairy armadillo. It is only about 6 inches (15 cm) long.

16. The largest is—you guessed it—the giant armadillo. This animal can grow up to 5 feet (1.5 meters) long.

17. A giant armadillo has up to 100 teeth.

18. Nine-banded armadillos always give birth to four identical babies.

19. The babies have soft carapaces when they are born. The carapaces get hard later on.

20. Armadillos can carry a rare disease called leprosy.

21. Only armadillos and humans can catch leprosy.

22. Armadillos use their sense of smell to find food.

23. They mostly eat beetles, insects, spiders, and grubs.

24. Sometimes they eat small reptiles and amphibians.

25. They also eat bird and reptile eggs.

26. Armadillos sleep up to 16 hours a day.

27. They are nocturnal and come out at night to find food.

28. People in South America used to make musical instruments out of armadillo shells.

ARCHER FISH

1. This fish looks normal enough. But it has a secret weapon for catching prey.

2. An archer fish can shoot a jet of water from its mouth.

3. It uses this super-soaker power to knock insects out of mid-air!

4. An archer fish can shoot down an insect up to 5 feet (1.5 meters) away.

5. An archer fish has a groove in the top of its mouth.

6. When it wants to shoot water, this fish pushes its tongue against the groove to form a tube, then pushes water down the tube and into the air.

7. An archer fish also has special eyes that can see straight ahead. This helps them see prey.

8. If an archer fish's water jet misses its prey, it can jump out of the water to catch the insect instead.

9. These fish are sometimes called "spitting sharpshooters."

10. Archer fish are about 9 inches (23 cm) long.

11. They live in swamps in Asia and northern Australia.

12. Some people keep archer fish in home aquariums.

ANGLERFISH

1. Anglerfish live deep in the sea.

2. They don't bother to hunt their prey. Instead, they wait for their prey to come to them.

3. Anglerfish have a rod on top of their head.

4. The rod has a tip filled with bacteria that glow in the dark.

5. The light attracts prey. When a fish swims too close, the anglerfish snaps it up.

6. An angler fish has a big mouth filled with very sharp teeth.

7. Its stomach can stretch out to hold fish more than twice its own size.

8. There are more than 200 species of anglerfish.

9. Some species of male anglerfish are tiny compared to females.

10. These males don't have the glowing rod to catch prey. Instead, they make females do all the work.

11. When a tiny male finds a female, it attaches itself to her body with its sharp teeth. Then it stays there for the rest of its life.

12. A female might have up to six males attached to her body.

ALLIGATOR SNAPPING TURTLE

1. This turtle is the largest species of freshwater turtle.

2. These bad boys (and girls) can weigh between 155 and 175 pounds (70 and 80 kg).

3. Rumor has it a 400-pound (180-kg) turtle was caught in Kansas in 1937, but no one can prove it.

4. Alligator snapping turtles only live in the United States.

5. Their spiky shells make them look like dinosaurs.

6. The alligator snapping turtle is the only species of snapping turtle with eyes on the sides of its head.

7. This turtle spends so much time lying still in the water that algae often grows on its shell.

8. It can stay underwater for up to 50 minutes before it needs a breath of air.

9. This turtle almost never goes on land.

10. Females go on land to lay their eggs.

11. Alligator snapping turtles lie motionless waiting for a fish to swim by.

12. The turtle's tongue looks like a red, wiggly worm. It waves its tongue back and forth to lure fish.

13. If a fish thinks the turtle's tongue looks like food, it will swim right into the turtle's jaws. Then—SNAP!—the turtle chomps down on its prey.

14. Alligator snapping turtles can also smell chemicals released by nearby fish. So even if a fish is hiding in the sand, the turtle will find it.

15. An alligator snapping turtle can bite down with a force of 1,000 pounds (454 kg). That's strong enough to crush bone!

16. These turtles lay their eggs in dirt mounds.

17. They lay up to 50 eggs in a clutch.

18. The temperature of the mound determines the sex of the babies.

19. Warm mounds produce female turtles. Cooler mounds produce males.

20. Baby turtles can take care of themselves as soon as they hatch.

AARDVARK

1. Even this animal's name is odd! Aardvark means "earth pig" in the Afrikaans language of South Africa.

2. Aardvarks are found all over Africa.

3. Aardvarks look a bit like pigs, but they are not related to them.

4. An aardvark has big ears like a rabbit.

5. Those big ears mean the aardvark has a great sense of hearing.

6. These animals dig burrows in the ground.

7. An aardvark's main burrow can be 30 to 40 feet (9 to 12 meters) long. • • • • • • • • • • • • • • • • • • •

8. Aardvarks walk on their toes.

9. Their front feet are shaped like shovels.

10. Aardvark claws are hard and tough, which makes them great for digging.

11. An aardvark's favorite foods are ants and termites.

12. Aardvarks use their feet to dig up termite mounds, then eat the insects inside.

13. They wiggle their long snouts to search for food.

14. Then they suck up termites and ants with their long, sticky tongue.

15. An aardvark's tongue can be almost 12 inches (30 cm) long.

16. Aardvarks also eat a plant called the aardvark cucumber.

17. When an aardvark poops out cucumber seeds, they grow into new plants.

18. An aardvark's back legs are longer than its front legs.

19. This mammal's body is covered with rough hairs.

20. An aardvark's tough skin protects it from ant and termite bites.

21. An aardvark can close its nostrils to keep out ants, termites, and dust.

22. Lions, leopards, cheetahs, hyenas, and pythons all like to eat aardvarks.

23. To escape from their predators, aardvarks run fast in a zigzag pattern.

24. Digging a burrow also provides a quick escape from danger.

25. Lions, hyenas, and other animals often move into abandoned aardvark burrows.

26. Aardvarks are nocturnal. They walk around all night looking for food.

27. An aardvark can eat up to 50,000 insects in one night.

28. Aardvarks are great swimmers.

29. Aardvarks only have a few teeth in the back of their mouths.

30. They swallow their food whole.

31. Aardvarks have the best sense of smell in the animal kingdom.

ODDBALL

FAST FACTS!

21 WEIRD AND WACKY PLANTS

Why should animals have all the fun? Plants can be pretty weird too, as this list shows.

1. **Hydnora:** This looks more like a horror-movie monster than a plant! The hydnora is a parasite. It grows underground and sucks up nutrition from the roots of other plants. Only the flower appears above ground, where it traps beetles so they can become covered with pollen, then releases the bugs to pollinate other plants.

2. **Rat-Eating Pitcher Plant:** It's not unusual for pitcher plants to catch bugs, but this variety has bigger plans. The 4-foot (1.2-meter)-tall plant is large enough to capture rats and other small rodents when they fall into the liquid-filled flowers. Then the strong acid inside digests the animals.

3. **Parachute Flower:** Insects think this plant smells good. But when they get too close, the insects are trapped inside. Once they are covered with pollen, the plant releases them.

4. Hammer Orchid: This Australian orchid is a trickster. It smells like a female wasp, which attracts male wasps. Once they touch the flower, the males discover their mistake—but not before they are covered with pollen, which they spread to other orchids.

5. Strangler Fig: This nasty parasite is no friend to other trees. The fig can grow downward, robbing the host tree's roots of nutrients. The fig also grows upward, blocking the sun and eventually killing its host.

6. Venus Fly-Trap: Any insect that comes too close to this plant's barbed leaves is in for a nasty surprise! The leaves close over the insect, trapping it inside, where it is eaten and digested.

7. Corpse Flower: Flowers are supposed to smell nice, right? Not the corpse flower, which stinks like a dead body. Why? The nasty smell attracts insects, which help pollinate the plant.

8. Sensitive Plant: This shy plant has an unusual defense. When anything touches it, its leaves close up. The plant does this by forcing water out of the leaf cells, which makes them collapse.

9. Death Apple Tree: Don't eat the apples from this tree! The fruit is poisonous, and the sap causes a burning reaction. Don't try to burn down this nasty plant, either—the smoke it would make is toxic too.

10. **Dancing Plant:** This plant just wants to have a good time! Found in Southeast Asia, the dancing plant responds to changes in light and movement, making it seem to dance.

11. **Rafflesia:** Another stinky plant, rafflesia have no stems, leaves, or roots. This plant's flower isn't just smelly—it's huge! A rafflesia flower can weight up to 24 pounds (11 kg).

12. **Flypaper Plant:** These weird plants give off a green glow to attract insects. But when mosquitos or other insects land on the sticky leaves, they become the plant's dinner!

13. **Lithops:** These plants have developed an oddball way to be left alone. Instead of looking like plants, they look like stones! Even scientists can be fooled by the lithops' clever camouflage. Lithops live in the desert in southern Africa, and if it doesn't rain, the plant gets all the water it needs from mist.

14. **Dead Horse Arum Lily:** This plant uses its nasty smell to trap insects, which then spread pollen to other plants. Even weirder—the lily is thermogenic, which means it produces its own heat to attract more insects.

15. **Dragon's Blood Tree:** This tree, which grows near Yemen, has a weird, umbrella-like shape. But it gets its name from the dark resin it produces, which looks like—you guessed it—a dragon's blood.

16. **Rootless Duckweed:** Say hello to the world's smallest flowering plant. This aquatic plant grows on the surface of ponds and lakes. Its flowers measure just $\frac{1}{32}$ of an inch (0.08 cm) wide.

17. **Doll's Eye:** The spots in the center of this plant's flowers make them look like doll's eyes, which is how the plant got its name. But don't be fooled—this plant's leaves, stems, and berries are poisonous.

18. **Monkey Face Orchid:** It's easy to see how this plant got its name—the center of its flowers looks just like a monkey's face. This plant grows in the high mountains of Ecuador and Peru and produces a scent that smells like oranges.

19. **Cobra Lily:** This plant got its name because it looks like a cobra snake ready to strike. And this plant lives up to its name! It gives off a scent that attracts insects, then catches and eats them by drowning them in its pitcher-shaped flowers.

20. **Rainbow Eucalyptus:** This tree grows in Papua New Guinea and gets its colorful appearance because its bark peels unevenly, revealing a variety of colors underneath.

21. **Baobab Tree:** The baobab is also called the "Tree of Life." It grows in the desert, and its huge trunk can store up to an astounding 1,000 gallons (3,785 liters) of water. Baobabs are also called "upside-down trees" because their thin branches and leaves are so high up the trunk. During droughts, elephants often rip into baobab trunks to get the water inside.

18

20